Twayne's United States Authors Series

Sylvia E. Bowman, *Editor*

INDIANA UNIVERSITY

Abraham Lincoln

ABRAHAM LINCOLN

By DAVID D. ANDERSON
Michigan State University

(TUSAS) 153

Twayne Publishers, Inc.   ::   New York

To Mother and Dad Rittenhour

Preface

THE PLACE of Abraham Lincoln in American literary history needs no justification; it has been secure since that afternoon in November, 1863, when Edward Everett, the orator of his day, acknowledged that his two-hour masterpiece had been surpassed by Lincoln's "Dedicatory Remarks," two minutes in duration. But the Lincoln of the Gettysburg Address, like the Lincoln of the "Rebecca letters," of the letter to Mrs. Bixby, and of the second inaugural address, has become lost in the mass of myth, folklore, scholarship, apocrypha, conjecture, and debate that has accumulated in the hundred years since his death. Although numerous attempts have been made to isolate the nature and substance of Lincoln's literary accomplishment from the complexity of the man, the President, and the legend, ultimately none has been satisfactory. Perhaps none can be. Yet, as testimony to the compelling nature of the task, the search for definition—of which this volume is a part—will continue.

The search begins—and sometimes stops—with acknowledgment of the complexity, the contrasts, the imponderability of the man, the curious fusion of realism and idealism in his personal and political philosophy and in his literary style. It looks for origins and influences, too frequently to take refuge in speculation or in the dubious memories of his contemporaries. It attempts to compare Lincoln's utterances with the acknowledged masterpieces of others, and often it has refurbished but not redefined the old clichés of "beautiful," "thought-provoking," and "inspiring." Or it bogs down in biography. Rarely, in studies that are inevitably too short as well as too general, one finds perception and insight that come close to what an ultimate definition must be. It can be attained only by use of all the tools available to the modern literary critic. Then, it must be acknowledged, it can be a definition only for our age.

However, the key to Lincoln's literary accomplishment was not found by a modern critic, but by one of his contemporaries who had observed him closely without intimacy throughout the four years of his Presidency, who sought to probe behind appearance and find reality, who sought to define reality in terms of both time and eternity. This man was Ralph Waldo Emerson, and his recognition of Lincoln as the Representative Man, the man who epitomized his own time and who transcended it to become timeless, is the point at which all literary criticism of Lincoln's work must begin and, perhaps, ultimately end.

Lincoln was a product of and representative of nineteenth-century America, of a time that sought a stormy balance between idealism and practicality as it defined and accepted a national identity. In many ways it anticipated the New Deal, the Fair Deal, the New Frontier, and the Great Society in its attempts to fuse real and ideal into a meaningful but practical whole. But these movements have been given direction and voice by intellectuals, scholars, and professional men of letters as well as by practical but compassionate politicians. In nineteenth-century American political life there were neither "brain trusters" nor "eggheads"; there were merely practical politicians, each of whom attempted to make his own sometimes dubious version of the ideal into the American reality. And each had to articulate his own vision.

From this political tradition came Lincoln and he, in Emerson's view, epitomized it completely. This tradition, on a more sophisticated, more admittedly pragmatic level, continues today; and to a great extent its impetus, as well as its inspiration, derives from Abraham Lincoln as it searches for national meaning in the guise of national identity and goals. Less evident, however, is the fact that to a great extent the political tradition parallels and often merges with the literary tradition that moved fumblingly, sometimes inarticulately, through the nineteenth century in its search for a parallel synthesis in meaning. Like the political tradition, the nation's literary tradition continues that search, perhaps more consciously artistic, more pragmatically professional, but with its roots firmly in the past.

Abraham Lincoln occupies a unique position at the center of both traditions as they fuse on the threshold of modern America. He was not a conscious literary artist, nor did he ever intend or attempt to be. Although he had a profound sensitivity and respect for words, he regarded them pragmatically, as means to the end of communication; and, as he searched deep within himself for the mystic faith and dedication with which he approached his political destiny, he searched also for the words with which to give form to his feelings.

The result was a contribution to the literary history of this country as unpretentious as it is profound, as meaningful in the twentieth century as it was immediate in the nineteenth. In the body of Lincoln's writings, ranging from fragments of verse and doggerel through military dispatches and political exhortations to the moments of poetic intensity and artistry in the Gettysburg Address and the Second Inaugural Address, there is an economy, a simplicity, and an appropriateness that demonstrate a fusion of form, idea, and emotion unduplicated in American literary history. At the same time, it is equally evident that at the heart of these writings there is an intrinsic fusion of faith and practicality, of vision and clear-sightedness, that makes them peculiarly American, both in their political and human immediacy and in the linguistic structures that give them permanence.

It is true that Lincoln's language, his ideas, his compassion, and his political philosophy have their origins in traditions far older than the United States—the Federal Union which to him symbolized his mystic faith in the dignity and worth of man. But the specific nature of each, like that of the country of which they are a part, was determined by the peculiar accidental combination of time, geography, nature, and human energy that became known as the American frontier. Although Lincoln transcended his origins, as all great men inevitably do, it was the social phenomenon of the frontier that made him possible, that gave form and substance to his innate intelligence and sensitivity at the same time that it permitted him to become Jefferson's natural aristocrat and eventually let him become Emerson's representative man. The commonness that becomes dignity, the ungainliness that becomes beauty, share the same qualities that permit bluntness and bawdy humor to become literature, just as out of the genetic clay of the West emerged greatness.

The magnitude of Lincoln the man, the symbol, and the myth makes examination of Lincoln the writer perilous; but my purpose is to build on previous achievements, to take warning of earlier defined pitfalls, and to define him as his works show him to be: a man who in the written word stands, as Emerson said in his memorial address in Concord on April 19, 1865, "an entirely public man; father of his country, the pulse of twenty millions throbbing in his heart, the thoughts of their minds articulated by his tongue," and who remained an entirely private man who felt more deeply and spoke more clearly than most of his countrymen have ever done. The tools of modern literary criticism are many and varied, and the works are worthy of them. I hope that the combination will, in this volume, lead to a more complete understanding of Lincoln the writer and perhaps, ultimately, to additional understanding of the man and his work.

DAVID D. ANDERSON

Lansing, Michigan

Acknowledgments

For the many kinds of assistance that contributed to the making of this book, I owe much gratitude: to the staffs of the Michigan State University Library, the State Library of Michigan, the Lansing Public Library, and the Rutgers University Press for their many courtesies; to Miss Janet Gassman for her customary excellent, critical typing; to Miss Sylvia E. Bowman for her usual editorial expertise; and again to my wife Pat for her encouragement, interest, patience, and help.

I am grateful, too, for another, less tangible kind of help that inspired me to attempt to penetrate the Lincoln myth and understand the man and the writer. Other Midwestern writers, among them Sherwood Anderson, Brand Whitlock, and Carl Sandburg before me, and my friends Russel Nye, T. B. Strandness, and William McCann, are to a great extent responsible for the existence of this study, because their interest and insights stimulated mine.

Chapter

Chronology

1809   Abraham Lincoln born on the Nolin River in Hardin County, Kentucky, on February 12, son of Thomas and Nancy Hanks Lincoln.

1811   The Thomas Lincoln family moved to a farm on Knob Creek.

1815–   Abraham Lincoln attended subscription A.B.C. schools
1816   for a few weeks each fall.

1816   The Thomas Lincoln family moved during the winter to Perry County, Indiana.

1820   Abraham Lincoln apparently attended Andrew Crawford's school, Spencer County, Indiana, for a few weeks during the winter.

1822   Attended "blab" school for about four months.

1824   Attended Azel Dorsey's school for about six months.

1827   Worked as farmhand and ferryman.

1828   Made first flatboat trip to New Orleans.

1829   Worked as store clerk.

1830   Moved with his family to Macon County, Illinois, where he became the "rail splitter."

1831   Made second flatboat trip to New Orleans.

1831   Arrived in New Salem, Illinois, by himself, a "piece of floating driftwood"; cast first vote; began to acquire local reputation as storyteller.

1832   Wrote platform as candidate for Illinois State Legislature; served as elected captain and later private of militia in the Black Hawk War, April–July; defeated for legislature; bought share of Berry's store.

1833   Became postmaster of New Salem, Illinois. Continued political activity.

1834   Became surveyor; elected representative to the legislature as Whig; studied law.

1836   Admitted to the Illinois Bar.

1837   Moved to Springfield; practiced law.

1842   Refused renomination to the legislature; the "Rebecca letters" published; married Mary Todd on November 4.

1843 Son Robert Todd Lincoln born on August 1.

1846 Elected to Congress on August 3; son Edward Baker Lincoln born on March 10.

1847– Member of Congress.
1848

1849– Practiced law in Illinois.
1860

1850 Edward Baker Lincoln died on February 1; son William Wallace born on December 21.

1853 Son Thomas Lincoln born on April 4.

1856 Presented as candidate for Vice Presidency in Republican National Convention on June 19.

1858 Nominated as Republican for U.S. Senator on June 16.

1858 Lincoln-Douglas debates, August–October; defeated for senatorship in November.

1859 Made speaking tour of Ohio, September. Wrote "Autobiography."

1860 Made Cooper Union address, February 28; spoke in New England, February–March; nominated as Republican candidate for the Presidency, May 18; elected sixteenth President of the United States on November 6.

1861 Farewell Speech to his friends in Springfield, February 11. Inaugurated President on March 4. War Message to Congress, July 4. Annual Message to Congress, December 3.

1862 William Wallace Lincoln died on February 21. President read first draft of preliminary Emancaption Proclamation to Cabinet on July 22. Letter to Horace Greeley, August 22. Completed second draft on September 17. Issued Proclamation on September 22, after Battle of Antietam. Annual Message to Congress, December 1.

1863 Signed Emancipation Proclamation on January 1. Wrote Gettysburg Address, November 17–19. Gave it at National Cemetery on November 19. Annual Message to Congress, December 9.

1864 Re-elected to the Presidency on November 8. Wrote letter to Mrs. Lydia Bixby on November 21. Annual Message to Congress, December 6.

1865 Inaugurated President on March 4. Shot on April 14, died on April 15.

CHAPTER 1

"The Short and Simple Annals . . ."

WHEN in June, 1860, Abraham Lincoln was asked for biographical information to include in campaign biographies, he demurred at first, turning to Thomas Gray's "Elegy Written in a Country Churchyard." There was not much to his early years, he insisted, except "the short and simple annals of the poor." The brief statement that he produced in response to repeated requests supports this contention in its sparse recital of biographical data.[1] What it does not include, however, is the fact that the Lincoln family experience, multiplied many times, was the American experience during the formative years of the country's existence. The peculiar manifestation of that experience that both shaped and in turn was partially shaped by the short and simple annals of the Lincoln family was what has become known as the American frontier.

Although the precise nature and extent of the frontier's impact on American life and thinking have been debated since Frederick Jackson Turner's classic statement in July, 1893,[2] there can be no question about the fact that it was and continues to be profound. Particularly important was the effect of that complex social, economic, political, and geographical movement upon the lives and thinking of its participants, among them the family of which Abraham Lincoln was a part. For the first twenty-two years of his life, Lincoln, in sharing the fortunes of his family, shared the experience of America's trek westward.

I *The Frontier Influence*

The frontier movement began centuries before and thousands of miles to the east of the frontier farm that Thomas Lincoln established on Nolin Creek in the new state of Kentucky; and, as it moved west across the Atlantic and a third of a continent, it carried with it ideas and ideals from both Europe and the Eastern coast of North America. But the American frontier—the movement that began with the establishment of a new nation on the Eastern coast of that continent—accepted as its ideological basis principles essentially European in origin that had been altered, re-emphasized, and given new meaning by the war out of which the new country had come, by the vision of an open society articulated by Thomas Jefferson, by the movement west itself, and by the new land beyond the Appalachian Mountains, much of the meaning of which came to be symbolized by Andrew Jackson.

The years during which Lincoln was part of the search for identity and permanence that was the frontier were crucial in making the ideal of the Revolutionary War a social, economic, and political reality. The country itself was seeking identity as a nation at the same time that it sought to define the relationship between the individual and the government that had been left unresolved by the war itself. At the heart of both searches was the attempt to resolve, in practical political activity within the framework of a republican political structure becoming increasingly democratic in its philosophy, a problem inherent in the political controversies that began before the revolutionary guns had cooled. This central problem was the attempt to determine the role of the individual in American life, and the direction in which a still elusive solution was to be found was to be pointed out by the men who sought their own personal destinies in the West. Among them was the obscure, insecure Thomas Lincoln.

With the election of 1800, often called the revolution of 1800, the conservative Adams-Hamilton faction fell into disrepute and disorganization, and the liberal Jeffersonian-Jacksonian philosophy that sought to expand the role of the individual began its forty years of domination. The result was a period of gradual but accelerating change in almost every area of American life—continued expansion of the franchise to more and more individuals, increased attempts at economic and social reform, and rapid geographic expansion across the Appalachians and on to the West. The Louisiana Purchase—damned as illegal and unconstitutional but nevertheless seen as necessary and inevitable by Jefferson—was a symbol of faith in man and in his progress toward perfectibility. In 1800 only one-twentieth of the population of the new country lived west of the Appalachians; by 1828 a third of the population had moved West. Almost to a man the settlers subscribed in whole or in part to the dominant liberal political philosophy, and each in his own way was consciously or unconsciously contributing to expanding the role of the individual in that increasingly vocal, increasingly politically powerful area in the heart of the continent.

The West was both unconscious symbol and harsh reality to the generation that crossed the mountains and to the generation that grew up in the new country. Like their ancestors who had crossed the Atlantic, each of them was fleeing from something in the stable, orderly society behind him; and each was seeking something in the unknown that lay to the west. Among these new generations were the grandparents—three of them, at least— and the parents, infants in their mothers' arms, of Abraham Lincoln. With them they carried from Virginia into Kentucky the genetic structure, about which much speculation and debate have centered, that was to produce Abraham Lincoln. More important and more relevant, they carried with them ideas, attitudes, and a religious faith, that, altered, redirected, and reemphasized in the area to the west, was to construct the environment out of which Lincoln came.[3]

II *The Parental Background*

Scholarly research, speculation, gossip, folklore, and myth have all contributed to the image of Lincoln's parents, Thomas Lincoln and Nancy Hanks, as that image has emerged out of the mist that is Kentucky in the ten years following its admission to the Union in 1796. Thomas Lincoln is both an ignorant, improvident wastrel and a careful, hard-working, but unlucky frontier craftsman-farmer; and Nancy Hanks is both a loose woman like her mother, and an honest, hard-working, God-fearing frontier wife and mother. Almost inevitably moral judgments imposed on both have been harsh, as they so frequently have been on their frontier contemporaries. But such judgments are almost without exception too righteously shortsighted in their refusal to acknowledge what the records, however incomplete, indicate, and what the results of their actions verify: these people pointed out the social and political direction that the country was to take, and they produced a succeeding generation capable of continuing in that direction.

As the available and not insignificant documentary evidence makes clear, Thomas Lincoln and Nancy Hanks combined in their marriage two important ingredients of the new frontier society. Thomas brought with him an intense, often aggressive democratic faith that manifested itself in civic responsibility as well as in confidence in himself, in his fellows, and in their combined ability to construct a meaningful and rewarding social and political structure. Unafraid of hard work, although often baffled by the due process of law, Thomas Lincoln gave his political allegiance to the party of Jefferson and his successor, Andrew Jackson, both of whom promised to provide a political and social atmosphere in which his hard work would be rewarded and in which law would become a means to that end rather than an obstacle to prevent its achievement.

Like the party that he supported, Thomas Lincoln subscribed to concepts of government and society that would have shocked his political mentor Jefferson but that pleased Andrew Jackson, the myth-ridden hero who came out of the West to succeed him. Thomas Lincoln was intensely individualistic, but his loyalties were to a federal rather than to a state or regional tradition; his economic beliefs were dynamic rather than stable; and his concept of the constitution was as a means to social and economic change rather than an instrument to prevent it. Within the framework of his democratic faith his movement westward was not improvident and aimless; it was optimistic, purposeful, and courageous.

To merge with and reinforce this political faith, Nancy Hanks brought to the marriage a religious faith equally simple, optimistic, and dedicated to individual responsibility for one's personal salvation. Like her husband, she was less concerned with denominational distinctions than with the message of truth; but she shared the evangelical Protestant faith that dominated the frontier as the Methodists and Baptists preached it on their circuits and in their camp meetings. Like Jacksonian democratic politics, this frontier variety of religion was intensely individualistic. Salvation was open to all; the clergy, who were of the people, could provide an atmosphere that would help the individual achieve it, but the ultimate responsibility was his own.

With unquestioning faith in the will and the omnipresence of God, the individual could work out his own destiny in the spiritual world as surely as in the temporal—with the help of God's grace and with the rejection of Satan's works.

III   *The Formative Years*

Into this environment, described later by Dennis Hanks as one in which "We lived the same as the Indians, 'ceptin' we took an interest in politics and religion," Abraham Lincoln was born on February 12, 1809. His first two years were spent in a small log cabin with a packed dirt floor, a single door and window, and a stick chimney. During these two years Thomas Lincoln farmed and did carpentry to earn a living, and he paid taxes and served on a jury. Apparently his future on the Nolin Creek farm, in spite of its stony soil, seemed as secure of any of his neighbors. At Nolin Creek, Abraham Lincoln learned to talk and to walk.

However, in the spring of 1811 Thomas Lincoln moved his family to a better farm on Knob Creek near Hodgenville, on the old Cumberland Road, the main route from Louisville to Nashville. Although the two hundred and thirty acres, much of it bottom land, were a great deal more promising, the physical features of the new cabin were no improvement over the old. Here the Lincolns lived for more than five years, until Thomas Lincoln decided to move on to southern Indiana; Lincoln's earliest memories were of the Knob Creek farm.

Kentucky and the West were rapidly being settled during these years; and, after the second war with England was won, the frontier in the Old Northwest was made reasonably secure from the Indians and the British traders and agitators from the Great Lakes country to the north. The Cumberland Road bore much of the increasing Western traffic: emigrants on their way to the Northwest, itinerant peddlers and preachers, soldiers going to and returning from Harrison's campaigns in the Northwest and from Jackson's in the South. If the frontier was a dynamic movement of restless, determined, pragmatic people essentially homogenous in culture and purpose, and rude, noisy, and energetic in accomplishment, the Cumberland Road provided a microcosmic view of it all. A great deal of folklore surrounds Lincoln's early childhood on the Knob Creek farm, all of it serving to accentuate what must have been an impressive experience for a boy growing into awareness with a wilderness behind him and its people at his door.

Less important, perhaps, as a contributor to the wealth of impressions that surrounded Lincoln's gradually emerging awareness in the Kentucky woods was his first experience at school, a certain sign that the Kentucky frontier was passing—that civilization, with its complexities, its search for order, and its dependence upon law to regulate both, was replacing the wilderness. In the fall of 1815, while Thomas Lincoln was defending in court his title to the Knob Creek farm, Abraham Lincoln and his sister Sarah, two years older, went to A.B.C. schools, or "blab schools" as they were known on the frontier. Subscription rather than free schools, they were taught by itinerant masters, many of them determined to make their marks in law, politics, or religion rather than in the gradually emerging educational structure of the frontier. The Knob Creek school was kept in the fall of 1815 by Zachariah Riney; in 1816, by Caleb Hazel.

Frontier pedagogy in the blab school was based upon discipline, memorization, and recitation. Even necessities, much less amenities, were almost nonexistent. The schoolhouse, often also a church, was a cabin usually smaller and more sparsely furnished than the children's homes; and the hazel switch wielded by the schoolmaster was the arbiter of decorum. Without books, slates, paper or pencils, memorization and recitation were the instruments of learning among the students of a wide variety of ages and ability. Moral principles, as Noah Webster, and William Holmes McGuffey made clear, were the proper substance of American education in the nineteenth century. It is impossible to determine what Lincoln learned in the Knob Creek blab school, but it is significant that forty-five years later, in the autobiographical fragment prepared for John T. Scripps, he recalled the names of both schoolmasters.

The complexities of securing and holding clear land titles in Kentucky were too much for Thomas Lincoln, as they were for many of his contemporaries. Although he had been appointed surveyor of that portion of the road in his vicinity and had been paying taxes on his property, the suit then pending against him over the Knob Creek farm sought to dispossess him. Perhaps as the result of confusion, frustration, and determination, he decided in the fall of 1816 to emigrate to Indiana Territory, where federal government guaranteed land titles could be had, where rich corn land could be purchased for two dollars an acre, and where both the Northwest Ordinance and the new state constitution declared that slavery, increasingly important in Southern agriculture, was to be forever prohibited. The Lincoln family became residents of free territory for the first time in December, 1816, at about the same time that that territory became a state.

Much has been made of the hardships of the journey and the first winter in Indiana, often as an indictment of Thomas Lincoln's character; but both were typical of the time, the place, and the circumstances. The Lincolns, no poorer than their neighbors, were not destitute. Thomas evidently traded his farm for four hundred gallons of whiskey, the cash commodity of the frontier; constructed a raft; and set off with the whiskey and the household goods down Knob Creek to Salt River and thence into the Ohio to locate and settle; he would then return for his family. But, plagued by the bad luck of the frontier as well as lack of skill in rafting, he upset his craft. Nevertheless, he accomplished his purpose; and in December the family was settled for the winter deep in the wilderness of Perry County, Indiana. Although the frontier had passed in Kentucky, the Lincolns caught up with it after a hundred-mile trip. They spent the winter in a three-sided temporary cabin; a more permanent residence would come later, with a formal claim to the land.

The almost fourteen years that the Lincoln family lived in southern Indiana were to a great extent repetitious of their years in Kentucky. Although tragedy intervened with the death of Nancy Hanks—a fate shared by many of their neighbors in the epidemic of 1818—Thomas Lincoln remarried a year later. Sarah Bush Johnson, a widow whom he had known in Kentucky, was, like Nancy Hanks, a devout revivalist with a firm faith in God, in religious experience, and in personal salvation as they were preached on the frontier. Unlike Nancy Hanks, she lived to old age and has emerged from the frontier mist as a person and a clearly defined influence during the formative years of young Abraham. A devout Baptist, a capable housekeeper, and a woman of strong opinions, she contributed a great deal to creating a home environment in which the young people—Thomas

Lincoln's two, her own three, and Dennis Hanks, an obscurely connected relative—could find their own destiny. Again family folklore and myth obscure the relationship between Abraham and his stepmother, but it remained close and sincere. In spite of her illiteracy she possessed a good mind and a sharp wit, as well as a sincere faith in individual responsibility. Often mystified by the boy Abraham, as she later admitted, she nevertheless protected and encouraged him.

Abraham Lincoln's years in Indiana were those during which he became a man; he was twenty-one when the family determined to move farther west to the corn country of the Illinois prairie, and he had determined to live not as a frontier farmer but as a townsman and to grow with the town. In Indiana, he recalled in his autobiographical fragment, he had begun almost at once to use the ax; and it was his major tool until he was twenty-three. He plowed, planted, harvested. Among his vivid memories were, at eight, shooting into a flock of wild turkeys and killing one, and at ten being kicked by a horse and "apparently killed for a time." Formal schooling during these years was scarce; yet he attended A.B.C. schools "by littles": in the winter of 1820, one kept by Andrew Crawford; in 1822, by James Swaney; and in 1824, for six months, his longest consecutive period of schooling, that of Azel Dorsey. At this point, his formal schooling—in aggregate just over a year—was finished.

IV Early Writing

From these years, and from the school experience, Lincoln's first efforts at writing are dated: the copybook doggerel verses like those inscribed by generations of schoolboys in their books, in Lincoln's case an arithmetic sum book he had made for himself. Of the fragments, three survive. Original composition is doubtful, and Albert J. Beveridge points out that one verse had perhaps been traditional in the Lincoln family. Taken together, however, they suggest, in addition to the schoolboy's erratic spelling and uncertain grammar, the emergence of blunt realism, in which fools are designated as such; of broad, unsubtle humor; and of a romantically poetic idealism—all three of them qualities that were to become integral parts of his personality, his speaking, and his writing:

> Abraham Lincoln his hand and pen
> he will be good but god knows When.
> Time What an emty vaper
> tis and days how swift they are
> swift as an indian arr[ow]
> fly on like a shooting star
> the presant moment Just [is here]
> then slides away in h[as]te
> that we [can] never say they[re ours]
> but [only say] they're past.[4]

In spite of the doubtful originality of these verses, a tradition unsubstantiated but attested to by William Herndon and several of Lincoln's old Indiana neighbors asserts that during these years Lincoln acquired minor local fame for writing "The Chronicles of Reuben," a satirical biblical parody poking fun at an alleged confusion of bedrooms at a local wedding. Furthermore, Herndon asserts that Lincoln composed a song, "Adam and Eve's Wedding Song," that was sung at the wedding of his sister Sarah in 1826, as well as a smattering of other doggerel verse, usually humorous and satirical, often bawdy, directed at persons and events in the Gentryville neighborhood. Although the editors of *The Collected Works of Abraham Lincoln* consider these episodes and the fragments collected by Herndon to be of such doubtful authenticity that they refuse to include them in the collection, it seems reasonable to assume that Lincoln, whose reputation as an avid reader during these years is unquestioned, had also become interested in writing.

V *Early Reading*

Lincoln's reading during these years was controlled but largely undirected by the nature of the frontier itself. Schoolbooks that found their way temporarily into his hands included Webster's *Spelling Book*, Dilworth's *Spelling Book*, and Murray's *English Reader*, all of them based upon an educational philosophy emphasizing sound moral standards as well as introducing the student to excerpts from great English prose and poetry. Herndon asserts that Lincoln cited the *English Reader* as the best school-book ever put into the hands of an American child. Still, however exciting these books were to him, the bulk of his early reading was done in stolen moments from borrowed books. But, in spite of the necessarily haphazard approach that he employed, his reading could not have been better focused if it had been planned and overseen in the schoolroom.

This reading included Aesop's *Fables*, which introduced him to the simple wisdom inherent in the commonplace; Scott's *Lessons in Elocution*, an introduction to Shakespeare and to oratory; and John Bunyan's *Pilgrim's Progress* and the King James Bible, introductions to the rhythm, strength, vigor, and vividness of English prose as well as stories of stark human drama. He read, too, Daniel Defoe's *Robinson Crusoe*, with its straightforward vigor, its fast-moving narrative, and its universal story of a lone individual's struggle against nature. For an imaginative boy growing conscious of the power and function of words, these works were heady stuff.

From the growing body of American history and biography he read Grimshaw's *History of the United States* and the lives of Washington by Weems and by Ramsey. The Weems biography, according to his own testimony, was the first book he had ever read through; and the Ramsey book was the basis for the Lincoln story known to every schoolboy: it had been damaged by rain while in his possession, and he spent two days pulling fodder for its owner in payment. Stylistically and historically unimportant, these books nevertheless brought home to him the meaning of human courage in relationship to his own country, and Weems in particular expressed that meaning in terms of human drama and determination, in language crudely but compellingly eloquent—so much so that Washington's crossing of the Delaware remained with Lincoln for years as a vivid drama that evoked in him a deep-seated, mystic patriotic sense of destiny.

Although he was later to deprecate the educational importance of these years in Indiana, stating that when he came of age he could "read, write, and cipher to the rule of three, but that was all," nevertheless the absorption of these books, word by word, rhetorical device by rhetorical device, stirring incident by stirring incident, magnificent human character by magnificent human character, provided the basis for an education both broad and deep, rooted firmly in the great deeds of brave and great men, and expressed in the most compelling language of the time and place. But this reading was only part of his education; it continued in the forests and fields and along the Mississippi River, in the Pigeon Baptist Church, and in the rabid Democratic political ferment of the age of Jackson.

VI *Religious Influences*

Stories abound concerning the impact on young Lincoln of the forests and fields as well as of his 1828 flatboat trip to New Orleans and return by land. But, although the relationship is evident, little is made of the influence upon him of frontier emotional religion and rowdy, dynamic politics. Both of them, however, were active interests of his father during the Indiana years; and both were rejected by the young Lincoln as he reached maturity. As an active member of the Pigeon Baptist Church together with his wife Sarah, Thomas Lincoln served on the discipline committee and as a trustee, positions not entrusted to those unwilling or unable to accept salvation or not able to evidence its achievement in their lives. To the Baptist of the early nineteenth-century frontier, faith meant not merely conscious acceptance of total immersion, but it demanded a personal conviction of sin; a public confession of faith, usually experienced through the prayers and exhortations of the minister; and a conscious acceptance of Christ as personal savior. It meant, too, that the individual must, through eschewing drinking, cursing, and other things of the devil, live an exemplary life. To the Baptist of 1828 this world was unimportant except as a preparation for the next; consequently, the means of attaining worldly prestige, particularly money and education, were not only unnecessary but often harmful and dangerous.

At the heart of this literal, fundamentalist creed lay the Bible, the word of God, and the intensely emotional transformation of that word into contemporary, meaningful exhortation through the revival techniques developed on the American frontier. The combination of the Word and the technique by a man of strong faith and voice who had personally felt both salvation and the call exerted a control over the close frontier community that extended into almost every aspect of human life. The permanence of that control is evident long after Lincoln's personal rejection of the creed in his refusal to drink or smoke as well as in the rarity with which he swore, even under the strongest provocation. To ascribe this pattern of behavior to personal fastidiousness in an age that considered these traits as manly, desirable vices is tenuous at best; it seems much more likely that the conviction of sin, ever present in the Lincoln household as well as in the Pigeon Baptist Church, had formed irreversible habits.

More important, however, than these personal habits upon Lincoln's thinking and ultimately upon his work was his concept of God—never in his adulthood defined through acceptance of a creed but evident in his pronouncements upon the meaning of man's lot. Lincoln, never completely the deist or agnostic that Herndon proclaimed him to be, regarded God in the last major speech of his life as the God of his Baptist youth—stern, unbending, righteous, He demanded the last full measure of blood in the expiation of man's sins. He also demanded that man acknowledge those sins and accept the punishment inherent in expiation.

VII *Political Influences*

In the Lincoln household Thomas Lincoln's political faith was as fervent as his religion, and during the campaign that led to Jackson's election in 1828 his son shared his fervor. Jackson was the Hero, the man larger than life who had come out of the West to champion the common man against the entrenched power of the East and to make Jefferson's dream of the open society a reality. In many respects, the political faith of the Democrats paralleled that of the frontier Baptists, especially in its view of man's lot.

The Jacksonian faith proclaimed that social and economic sin must be acknowledged and expiated; it believed that the individual must work out his social and economic destiny for himself, that government can help, but that the final responsibility must be his own. It preached, too, faith in the Declaration of Independence, literally interpreted to mean equality of opportunity and translated in practical terms into economic equality. Suspicious of central authority, it nevertheless exhibited a mystic reverence for the collective will of the people as manifested by their Jacksonian instrument, the federal government, and by the personification of that collective will in Andrew Jackson himself.

These principles, too, were carried by Lincoln into Whiggery and later Republicanism. Although he later rejected Jackson as leader and as symbol, he accepted the democratic reality for which Jackson stood on the frontier. The personality of Jackson himself had been the overwhelming issue of the election of 1828 in Indiana, as in the rest of the West. Behind that symbolic issue stood the people and the nation as opposed to the sectional and economic interests of Eastern minorities who still sought, in the name of a defunct Federalism and emerging Whiggery, to disregard the will and to minimize the power of the frontier masses.

Jackson carried Indiana by more than five thousand votes; and he was assisted, as Herndon cites Mrs. Crawford's memories, by young Abraham Lincoln's lusty version of an old campaign song that evoked the personality of the Hero. But more important to Lincoln's emerging political consciousness was the frontier political platform behind Jackson: an expansion of the franchise to include more and more freeborn whites, not excluding women; a central government ultimately strong enough to provide the aid demanded by this mass electorate; a constitution flexible enough to provide a legal basis for expanded assistance; an egalitarian society; a view of politics as a practical, expedient means of accomplishing the public will; a reverence for individualism encouraged but in no way inhibited by government; an acceptance of geographic, social, and economic mobility that transcended state boundaries as easily as it ignored the class stratification of the American past and the American East.

Indiana was, in the 1820's, a microcosm of the frontier as, through the growth of the democratic process, it groped its way toward order and stability and moved toward a national identity through a close personal relationship with the symbol of national government. But, as the frontier moved toward order, it served as a testing ground in which the direction of mobility was determined by the talents, abilities, and determination of the inhabitants. Consequently, the very weak and the very strong— those who had either been rejected by the system or who had ridden it to power—remained behind, caught up by increasing rigidity and conservatism. But those who were neither, who still combined the restlessness of the frontier with its dream, continued to move west, toward the still open society and toward land that was still free. Among them was the Lincoln family.

In February, 1830, just after Abraham Lincoln's twenty-first birthday, the move was begun. Like the move to Indiana, this one was considered to be permanent, a move to the rich corn prairies of central Illinois. A state for twelve years, Illinois, in spite of its Black Laws, was free politically and socially; it was strongly democratic; and it, too, was moving toward order and stability. Both Thomas Lincoln and his son saw it as a land of opportunity, but Thomas carried with him implements to break the virgin soil, whereas Abraham laid in a supply of trinkets to peddle to frontier housewives on the way. By ox-pulled wagon they went, repeating the Indiana experience as they located land near Decatur, built a cabin, and split rails for a fence. But the land was not wooded bottom land and hills; it was open prairie.

CHAPTER 2

"A Piece of Floating Driftwood . . ."

LATER in July, 1831, Abraham Lincoln arrived in New Salem, Illinois, a village on the Sangamo River. Twenty-two years old and almost penniless, he had no skills except those of the frontier, although he could read and write. But hard work and piety or even faith in Andrew Jackson had done little for his father, and Lincoln had made an important decision. He was determined to become a townsman, one of those, it seemed, who profited most by social and economic mobility while they sought geographic stability. In his move to New Salem, Lincoln rejected the economic and religious faith of his father; in a short time, he was to reject his politics also. Still psychologically a frontiersman, however, he was seeking a new frontier, that which the old frontier had made possible, but which later in the nineteenth century was to distort the meaning of the old frontier in the name of its heritage.

Lincoln's years in New Salem contributed much to the Lincoln myth and to the development of Lincoln as political realist, as logician, and as effective user of the English language. There he began his political career and the study of law, the two forces that shaped both his thinking and his prose style. There, too, the documentary record—the essays, speeches, and statements in which he developed both thinking and style—began to replace the myth of his developing years.

Before coming to New Salem, Lincoln had built the base of his later reputation as rail splitter and he had traveled again to New Orleans, but these activities had intensified the experiences of the past. In New Salem his directed, determined education began, building upon rather than replacing what he had learned as a youth. He came there, as he later commented, intending to stay and to learn a necessary trade that would enable him to grow with the frontier community that, like other frontier towns, promised so much to its residents. In 1831 New Salem was inhabited by a dozen families, it occupied a fever-free site on a hill just above a potentially navigable river—as almost all rivers on the frontier were considered potentially navigable—and it had a mill. Like Chicago to the north, it was, in 1831, a village with an apparently promising future.

Lincoln had a job in prospect as clerk in charge of Denton Offut's new store, and in considering his future prospects he thought of both blacksmithing and the law. Because of his limited education the former seemed more likely, but in any event he was determined to be a townsman. As a literate, increasingly articulate young resident during the 1830's, he drifted tentatively but perhaps inevitably into politics, first combined with storekeeping and then with surveying. Ultimately, however, in keeping with an emphasis rapidly becoming an American tradition, he determined to combine politics with the law.

A frontier political career demanded not only literacy, but, in the Jacksonian manner, a close identification with the democratic electorate; and Lincoln possessed both. His reputation as a storyteller and as a backwoods strongman began early in his New Salem residency, and his literacy made him invaluable as an election clerk and as witness and drawer of deeds and agreements. In March, 1831, his reputation in the community was strong enough to permit him to declare his candidacy for representative in the Illinois State Legislature, and in April he was elected captain of the local militia company as it set off to meet the last Indian threat to Illinois in the Black Hawk War. But in August, despite his growing reputation and the military service that he was later to treat as a frontier joke, he was defeated for the legislature—the only time, despite his increasingly outspoken Whig political views, that he was to be defeated in a direct popular election.

For the six years of his New Salem residency Lincoln continued to earn his living as a storekeeper, a surveyor, and later a representative in the legislature. But his accomplishment was not so important in these years as his apprenticeship. His instinctive rejection of the politics, religion, and way of life of his father gained support in his logic, increasingly sharpened by his growing familiarity with the law and by his steadily and consciously pursued mastery of the language. The New Salem years were marked for Lincoln by a growing ambition for security and respectability, by an increasingly powerful conviction that reason rather than emotion was necessarily at the heart of successful human relations, and by a pragmatic, rationally controlled intellectual curiosity.

His conversion to Whiggery shortly after his arrival in New Salem was both the result of and symptomatic of those qualities. Nationally a minority party, as it was on the frontier, the Whig party emerged slowly as a loose amalgamation of conservatives and anti-Jackson men. On the frontier, it was held to be the party of wealth and special interests. Lincoln attributed his own conversion, hardly a pragmatically wise decision, to reading Henry Clay's speeches in the Louisville *Journal*. Clay's eloquence, humanitarianism, patriotism, and rationality were particularly compelling, as Lincoln later acknowledged in his eulogy of Clay. Equally important, however, was Clay's practical stand on internal improvements for the West and his evidence in his own career that education, respectability, and reason could lead to a successful career west of the mountains as easily as in the East. In making this political move, Lincoln not only cut a major tie with his past and his surroundings, but he cast his lot with the eighteenth-century ideal of a natural aristocratic leadership of a society open and democratic—and he determined to be one of those leaders. He sought, too, orderly, harmonious, gradual progress economically and socially for the society in the West as it moved toward that ideal. He accepted as the basis of his political philosophy human values rationally defined and argument based upon reason rather than bombast. Above all, he accepted as a goal an elusive human dignity both for himself and for others.

These political changes meant that he cut himself off from the political faith of his father and his youth, but they did not mean that he accepted a synthetic aristocracy as he was later accused of doing, and his ties with the people—except his father—remained close. He had chosen a path to achieving the democratic ideal different from that followed by Jackson and his neighbors, and the people of Sangamon County recognized that he had. Never reconciled with his father or his stepbrother John D. Johnston, both of whom he considered dominated by the Jacksonian evil that rejected individual responsibility, he never severed his ties with the people, either of Sangamon County or of the country that he began increasingly to see in mystic union with its people.

Like his political faith, the religious faith that dominated the rest of his life undoubtedly dates from these years. Unlike his father and stepmother, he had never been admitted to membership in the Baptist Church; but during his youth, in a time during which many young men had not yet experienced conversion, that would have been no real cause for alarm. But he never did become a church member; and, although Herndon and James Matheny were firmly convinced that he was an infidel, perhaps an atheist, his rejection of religion seems to have been restricted to sectarianism and perhaps to the divinity of Christ. He seems, as suggested by his devotion to the Bible as a source of inspiration as well as his constant reverent references to God and nature, to have turned to the eighteenth century for his religious as well as his political faith and to have become in spirit a Unitarian but not a complete Deist. Certainly his fundamentalist faith in and awe of God as creator and as source of justice remained, to re-emerge in moments of crisis in later years.

His decision to turn to the law as a means of respectable livelihood was related to and perhaps partially responsible for his rejection of the political and religious structures of his youth. For the son of a frontier farmer to turn to the law was little less heretical than for him to reject revivalism and Jacksonianism. Like Whiggery and infidelity, the law was evil; but it had the distinction of being a necessary evil. The frontier attitude toward the legal structure of an orderly society was clearly defined by James Fenimore Cooper's Natty Bumpo: the law provided a dangerous weapon for the shrewd and unscrupulous to employ against the unwary, unschooled individual. Such had been Thomas Lincoln's experience in common with his fellow frontier farmers. Always eager to sue, convinced that somehow justice was possible, they nevertheless were equally convinced that legality was trickery and showmanship rather than rationality and harmony. Thomas Lincoln, like many others, moved westward as much in search of uncomplicated legal structures as in search of fertile land. But the lawyer was necessary to bring order if not justice to a land that had never known either.

Perhaps drawn to the law at first as a respectable, literate profession, as a means to understanding the mystery that entangled his fellows, or as an adjunct to a political career, the evidence suggests that, from his first days in New Salem, Lincoln was attracted to the documents of law that made order out of chaos and to the clear, unambiguous logic of language that made those documents possible. Although he gained a reputation for the shrewdness and showmanship essential to a law career in the American tradition then coming into being, his arguments increasingly began to demonstrate a conviction that law is the language of reason and, consequently, of justice. Not above either shrewdness or showmanship in his legal and political career—even to the extent of growing a beard at the behest of a child whom Lord Charnwood rightly characterized as insufferable—nevertheless both techniques quickly became subordinate means. Consequently, although he permitted himself to become the Rail Splitter, he early became and remained Honest Abe. His reputation for storytelling became a legend, but so did his veracity. To him, the law was above all a search for justice through reason, just as politics, the instrument that produces law in a democratic society, was a search for the means whereby equality before the law could become a realizable ideal.

Both the facts and the legends that have come out of Lincoln's years in New Salem indicate that his ambition, reason, and pragmatism led to his major decisions of those years; to the shape they took as they became reality; and to his continuing emphasis upon learning and particularly on language as the instrument of communication, of persuasion, of reason, and of justice. Storytelling in the idiom and dialect of the frontier was not merely humorous and entertaining, he learned, but effective and consequently pragmatic, whether around a campfire on the trail of Black Hawk or in a country tavern; and the language of law and reason was no less effective, as his reading of Henry Clay made evident to him. Both legend and fact, so often fused through Herndon's diligent devotion, agree that Lincoln learned in New Salem to use language effectively and appropriately; but much of the means of his doing so is still open to speculation.

Nevertheless, he read widely and he studied consciously, following a plan little less rigid, although much more haphazard, than that devised by Benjamin Franklin a century before. Along with Lincoln's growing reputation for storytelling, his reputation as an omnivorous reader became part of New Salem's folk-lore; and both storekeeping and surveying, the professions of his New Salem years when the legislature was not in session, gave him the time to read and the mobility to seek out books in the neighborhood. His brief stint as postmaster gave him free access to newspapers, particularly to the Louisville *Journal* which was important in developing his Whig faith.

Debate and speculation continue over the degree and source of direct instruction in grammar given Lincoln in New Salem, but William Dean Howells and subsequent scholars give the honor to Mentor Graham, in spite of Graham's often erratic spelling and syntax. But perhaps more realistic—in terms of Lincoln's statement to Squire Godbey quoted by Herndon, that "I'm not reading—I'm studying"—is the assumption that Lincoln's determined if admittedly imperfect assault on English grammar according to the principles set forth by Samuel Kirkham's *Grammar,* an "English Grammar in Familiar Lectures, Accompanied by a Compendium, Embracing a New Systematized Order of Parsing," was largely self-directed. Lincoln, quickly mastering its prescriptions, passed on to practice writing diligently in search of a style as clear, simple, and concise as he could make it. Perhaps Graham directed him to a borrowed copy of Kirkham, but the work seems to have been his own.

I *The First Political Document*

Although the course of self-improvement in writing that Herndon and his informants insist Lincoln followed in New Salem parallels that of Franklin without the use of Addison and Steele as models, no verified exercises of the period survive. But his first surviving political document, drawn up to announce his candidacy and platform for election to the legislature in March, 1832, indicates that his studying was already making its impact on his writing. Dated March 9 and published in the *Sangamo Journal* on March 15, 1832, the document focuses upon the need for internal improvements, a cardinal tenet of his newfound Whiggery, and specifically upon making the Sangamon River navigable. But especially important in the document are the carefully reasoned explorations of the subject and the clear simplicity with which they are phrased. The organizational pattern is logical and clear, with a general introduction, followed by the discussion of both the problem and the necessary practical financial basis for internal improvements, and then acknowledgment of other pressing problems—the regulation of usury and the need for education—followed by a humble, self-effacing conclusion. Direct, simple, reasoned, and clear, the announcement stands in marked contrast to the extravagant promises, the not-infrequent bombast, and the eloquent but meaningless perorations of most of his contemporaries. Indicative of the restraint, the lucidity of the style, and the practical reasoning of the approach to the subject is this early paragraph:

> Time and experience have verified to a demonstration, the public utility of internal improvements. That the poorest and most thinly populated countries would be greatly benefitted by the opening of good roads, and in the clearing of navigable streams within their limits, is what no person will deny. But yet it is folly to undertake works of this or any other kind, without first knowing that we are able to finish them—as half finished work generally proves to be labor lost. There cannot justly be any objection to having rail roads and canals, any more than to other good things, provided they cost nothing. The only objection is to paying for them; and the objection to paying arises from the want of ability to pay.[1]

In syntax and in flavor there is much of the frontier in this document, as there was to be in many of Lincoln's writings to the end. But even at this date that atmosphere was subordinate to the mind, the source of reason, and to words, the means whereby reasoned thought can be communicated. More important, however, is the indication that Lincoln had already refused to indulge in either the rhetorical flourishes that characterized much political oratory of the period or the frontier bombast exploited in the name of Davy Crockett.

Particularly apparent in the document are the personal humility and the willingness to occupy the reasoned middle ground that were to continue to characterize his personal writing and many of his political statements except in the later instances of biting sarcasm and satire. In the final two paragraphs, those which the rhetorical textbooks insist are remembered by a reader or listener, reasoned humility prevails, but not in the manner of a textbook exercise. Instead the style is that of a modest man determined not to be misunderstood:

> ... Considering the great degree of modesty which should always attend youth, it is probable I have already been more presuming than becomes me. However, upon the subjects of which I have treated, I have spoken as I thought. I may be wrong in regard to any or all of them; but holding it a sound maxim, that it is better to be only sometimes right, than at all times wrong, so soon as I discover my opinions to be erroneous, I shall be ready to renounce them. (I, 8)

In intensely personal and candid terms the last sentence emphasizes his willingness to accept the decision of the electorate, and at the same time it skillfully reminds that electorate of his kinship with them. But again humility prevails: "But if the good people in their wisdom shall see fit to keep me in the background, I have been too familiar with disappointments to be very much chagrined" (I, 9). Acceptance of reality, apparent in this first political document, was to remain a basic characteristic of Lincoln's writing and his thinking, but the poetic qualities that transcend reality and seek a meaning beyond it were far in the future. In this first political statement his words were designed to clarify; to communicate his thinking directly and simply, perhaps as much to himself as to the voters; and to convey something of himself.

This statement was prepared before Lincoln had intensified his campaign of self-education, particularly in the law; but, when the personal references are deleted, it has much of the lucidity that Lincoln had begun to admire and imitate. In its final preparation, however, the grammatical errors to which he was addicted were apparently removed by James McNamar, perhaps the best educated among the young men of New Salem and later the third person in the Ann Rutledge story. But the document itself, in its sentiments and in its acceptance of Clay's Whig principles, is unequestionably Lincoln's.

The Black Hawk War, intervening between Lincoln's declaration and the election, was, as Lincoln later described it, largely a lark for the New Salem troops; and, in the election almost immediately after they were discharged, Lincoln, although carrying his home district, was, perhaps fortunately, defeated. In the next two years he continued to earn his living by storekeeping and surveying, but his major interest had become self-education. In those two years he discovered the ordered reason and the lucid prose of the eighteenth century in a second-hand copy of Blackstone's *Commentaries on the Laws of England.* Not only was the study of Blackstone essential to the young man who aspired to be a lawyer, but it gave impetus to his search for the ultimate in clarity and order in his own writing. Like Franklin, Lincoln recognized intuitively, with the appreciation of one with a natural affinity for words and for reasoned analysis, Blackstone as a master of both. Blackstone provided him with example and inspiration, and he pursued both relentlessly.

Supplementing his discovery of Blackstone were his reading of Gibbon's *The Decline and Fall of the Roman Empire* and his mastery of the mathematics of surveying. From Gibbon he learned more of logic, order, harmony, and clarity in expression; and from both Gibbon and mathematics he learned precision and the techniques of cool, objective appraisal, an appreciation of the beauty inherent in form, and a conviction that order can be found and expressed through language. A product of the American geographical frontier, Lincoln had inadvertently found his teachers in an age that sought the rational frontiers of the mind.

In Lincoln the natural affinity of each of these frontiers for the other came together, and each reinforced the other in his thinking and his writing. Both eighteenth-century rationalism and the American frontier experience were firmly rooted in objective reality, and each sought to make order and harmony out of apparent chaos. Surveying and the law were the means by which the geographic frontier was to become civilized, characterized by the order which Thomas Lincoln had found so elusive; and the rationalism of the eighteenth-century Enlightenment sought a higher natural order based upon emulation of the observable laws of the universe. To the eighteenth-century mind, that ultimate order was manifested in the natural rights necessary to the achievement of human dignity; but that characteristic had eluded the Lincoln family as they, like their Western contemporaries, flirted constantly and unwillingly with the specters of destitution and degradation.

These rational influences, attractive to Lincoln's analytical mind and to his natural practicality, were superimposed on the major influences of his boyhood, the emotional attachments to Jacksonian politics and fundamentalist religion; and the domination of mind over emotion threatened to obliterate the earlier influences, products of a time and experience he had repudiated. But increasingly, with maturity and experience, a balance was struck, only rarely to become stormy and threatened under the impact of crisis.

Important to Lincoln's growth during these years was a natural characteristic developed through exercise that gave impetus to his political career at the grassroots of Sangamon County and that later contributed to his ability to maintain that sometimes precarious balance. This sense of humor—blunt, practical, and even bawdy—combined with his storytelling ability to make him known, liked, and understood in the rough political tradition of the frontier. Like his rationalism in religious matters, Lincoln's humor has taken its place in the Lincoln myth to the consternation of political and moral apologists. But more important was its role in his career and in his thinking, and it remains as an appealingly human quality that has made impossible the persistent efforts to dehumanize and to deify him.

Firmly rooted in the harsh irony of practical frontier experience, Lincoln's humor manifested itself in a lively contrast to the often-noted romantic, uncertain melancholy of his young manhood—a characteristic ascribed by Herndon to his alleged romance with Ann Rutledge in New Salem and made much of by the mythmakers. As contemporary accounts make clear, when Lincoln took the political stump or began to tell a story, his features were lifeless, the result, according to the mythmakers, of his melancholy. But that inanimation quickly disappeared, and Lincoln became an actor, alive in both speech and actions as he mimicked, imitated, and parodied his subject or became engrossed in his speech. His humor was blunt and barbed and his satire and sarcasm often curiously insensitive as when, on at least one occasion, he reduced his political opponent to tears; and, after another, he was challenged to a duel. But no verified examples of his early humor or satire survive.

II *The Political Documents of 1836*

Nor do authentic documents survive from Lincoln's second,

successful campaign for the Illinois state legislature in 1834, but two from his successful campaign for re-election in 1836 make evident the blunt, rational simplicity of his Whiggery and the subtle sharpness of his ironic wit. Both qualities were of inestimable value in his success, admired as they were in the context of the Jacksonian faith of the constituents who elected him. In his own narrow field Lincoln had begun to contribute to the growing inroads made by Whig frontier politicians on the Democratic stronghold; he was, in effect, a local manifestation of shrewd and necessary Whig national policy.

The first of the documents, a letter of 1836 to the editor of the *Sangamo Journal,* is a platform statement that makes clear the mixture of revolutionary and conservative sentiment that characterized Lincoln's Whiggery. At the same time it contrasts with his statement of four years before in its direct, simple abruptness and in its obvious self-confidence. No longer a humble, inexperienced office seeker, Lincoln at twenty-five was a two-year veteran of the legislature; and he was soon to be admitted to the bar. The letter suggests that Lincoln was not only aware of his qualifications but that he was close to being brash. But, as in the earlier statement, Lincoln was again scrupulously clear, although his earlier naïve formality had been replaced by a fresh colloquialness.

To the Editor of the Journal: New Salem, June 13, 1836

In your paper of last Saturday, I see a communication over the signature of "Many Voters," in which the candidates who are announced in the Journal, are called upon to "show their hands." Agreed. Here's mine!

I go for all sharing the privileges of the government, who assist in bearing its burthens. Consequently I go for admitting all whites to the right of suffrage, who pay taxes or bear arms, (by no means excluding females).

If elected, I shall consider the whole people of Sangamon my constituents, as well those that oppose, as those that support me.

While acting as their representative, I shall be governed by their will, on all subjects upon which I have the means of knowing what their will is; and upon all others, I shall do what my own judgement teaches me will best advance their interests. Whether elected or not, I go for distributing the proceeds of the sales of the public lands to the several states, to enable our state, in common with others, to dig canals and construct rail roads, without borrowing money and paying interest on it.

If alive on the first Monday in November, I shall vote for Hugh L. White for President.

Very respectfully,
A. LINCOLN
(I, 48)

The simple, informal logic of Lincoln's platform, reinforcing his personal popularity and reflecting the national strategy of the Whigs to break the Jacksonian hold on the frontier, was successful. Not only did he lead the slate of seventeen candidates for the legislature, seven of whom, all Whigs, were elected; but Senator White of Tennessee, the Whig Presidential candidate, carried Sangamon County. However, a national victory for the Whigs was still four years off. As the letter indicates, for Lincoln a logical platform fused the frontier demand for a broad, unrestricted franchise—traditionally a democratic token of faith in the common man—with recognition of the need for a vast program of public-supported internal improvements, both of which were balanced by the traditional conservative demand for fiscal control and responsibility.

The second document that survives from this campaign, a letter privately written and sent to a political rival, reflects, behind a mask of modest diffidence, a remarkably sophisticated and controlled irony. Addressed to Colonel Robert Allen, who had implied that he had secret knowledge that would insure the defeat of Lincoln and Ninian Edwards at the polls but that he withheld it out of regard for Lincoln, the letter is not indicative of Lincoln's "candor, honor, and high integrity"[2] as much as it reflects the impact of his eighteenth-century reading upon a sense of irony razor sharp. Like Swift's "A Modest Proposal," the letter masks righteous indignation with earnest naïveté. Only at the end does Lincoln permit the mask to slip and the reality of his outrage at injustice become evident. The letter begins in fact: "I am told that during my absence last week, you passed through this place, and stated publicly, that you were in posession of a fact or facts, which, if known to the public, would entirely destroy the prospects of N. W. Edwards and myself at the ensuing election; but that, through favor to us, you should forbear to divulge them" (I, 48–49).

Then, with modest candor and moral righteousness, Lincoln went on:

> No one has needed favours more than I, and generally, few have been less unwilling to accept them; but in this case, favour to me, would be injustice to the public, and therefore I must beg your pardon for declining it. That I once had the confidence of the people of Sangamon, is sufficiently evident, and if I have since done any thing, either by design or misadventure, which if known, would subject me to a forfeiture of that confidence, he that knows of that thing, and conceals it, is a traitor to his country's interest. (I, 49)

Then Lincoln turned to honest bewilderment and assurances of confidence in Allen: "I find myself wholly unable to form any conjecture of what fact or facts, real or supposed, you spoke; but my opinion of your veracity, will not permit me, for a moment, to doubt that you at least believed what you said" (I, 49). With almost servile gratitude for Allen's regard and faith in his integrity, he continued: "I am flattered with the personal regard you manifested for me, but I do hope that, on more mature reflection, you will view the public interest as a paramount consideration, and therefore, determine to let the worst come" (I, 49).

Mock resignation, pseudo-sincere reassurances, and a final blunt, unmasked challenge mark the concluding paragraphs of the letter:

> I here assure you, that the candid statement of facts, on your part, however low it may sink me, shall never break the tie of personal friendship between us.
> I wish an answer to this, and you are at liberty to publish both if you choose.
>
> Verry Respectfully,[3]
A. LINCOLN.
(I, 49)

Such a sustained ironic tone indicates that Lincoln had mastered the satiric spirit of his eighteenth-century masters in the four years since he first modestly placed his candidacy before the electorate of Sangamon County. No longer the uncertain, unsophisticated country boy, Lincoln had, by 1836, acquired a mastery of political adaptability and levels of language usage that for almost thirty years marked his legal and political speaking and writing. Combined, these two documents of 1836 illustrate the remarkable range of his language and literary style at twenty-five: in the first, a firm grasp of the blunt, direct colloquial language, marked by an air of jovial eagerness, that was manadatory on the political stump of the Illinois prairies; and, in the second, a restrained, subtle control of ironic indignation almost unknown in the political annals of the frontier and yet unmistakably forceful in its emphasis. By the fall of 1837 Lincoln had not only served his legal apprenticeship; he had served much of his literary apprenticeship as well.

Unfortunately, the texts of his political speeches of these campaigns no longer survive; but recollections collected by Herndon and partisan reports from the *Sangamo Journal* agree that Lincoln was as effective on the stump as he was in both of these letters. Invariably, he began with an air of modest embarrassment; but, as he proceeded, he became eloquently alive and certain as, through logical directness, careful delineation of facts, and a ready wit that ranged from drollery to satire, he stated his own position and demolished that of the opposition. Never one to evade an issue or to leave an opponent's argument unshredded, Lincoln provided much delight for his partisan audiences in an age and time that demanded both a sound position and a good show.

By the fall of 1836, when he was admitted to the bar, Lincoln was characterized by the paradoxes in his nature that dominated his writing and his relations with others until they became incorporated in the Lincoln myth. Awkward and uncouth in appearance, he was nevertheless graceful and forceful in action; modest and diffident, he was blunt and forthright; and melancholy and uncertain though he frequently was, in a moment he could be rollicking with humor, often droll, but, almost as often, bawdy and practical. Strongly emotional, he was in his public writing and speeches coolly and intellectually controlled.

The young Lincoln seems to have been confident that in the open society of rural, frontier Illinois he could make a place for himself; and, since New Salem seemed to be slipping into the limbo into which so many frontier towns disappeared, he did not hesitate to abandon it for the thriving city, soon to be the state capital, at Springfield. Although his arrival there on April 15, 1837, was humble enough, it was, however, as a member of the bar and of a practicing law firm that he came. He was no longer the piece of floating driftwood that had come to New Salem five years before; and, as when he had left his family to make his way in the world he did not look back. There is no suggestion of human compassion or of nostalgic regret in the surviving writings of the confident young lawyer.

CHAPTER *3*

"... he ... removed to Springfield, and commenced the practice ..."

S PRINGFIELD, ILLINOIS, was to be Lincoln's home for the
rest of his life; he arrived there in 1837 as an ambitious
young lawyer-legislator, and he left in 1861 as the President-
elect of the United States. The intervening years made that rise
possible, perhaps even inevitable, as they contributed to the
development and consolidation of his thinking, the maturation
of his emotions, and the skill with which he attacked and laid
bare the issues of those crucial years. During those years nineteenth-century America fumbled toward a social and political
identity that would bring the ideals of the eighteenth century
closer to the reality of a society in which frontier mobility was
rapidly passing and in which a new mobility, based on a new
concept of the role of government, particularly the federal government, had to be forged. The years Lincoln spent in Springfield made possible his crucial role in that revolution, and as a
result they have given substance to the American myth propagated by Horatio Alger and the Lincoln myth, brought into
being by those who sought to understand the profound impact
of the man on his times. As Lincoln's years in Springfield suggest, both myths have their origins in reality.

In the final months of his New Salem years and in the first
of his Springfield residency he made clear two points of view,
one intensely personal and the other a matter of public record,
that were to have profound effects on the outcome of those
Springfield years. Unfortunately, however, the significance of
both has largely been ignored by those who seek to penetrate
the Lincoln myth, although both are adequately documented.
The first is his love affair with Mary Owens, insight into which
is provided by a series of letters written to her by Lincoln; the

second is his statement on slavery, presented to the state legislature on March 3, 1837. Combined, they make clear the ambiguity and dichotomy of Lincoln as man and politician; and they also show the combination of certainty and uncertainty with which Lincoln approached decisions. Problems which dealt with human beings in the abstract could be intellectualized and resolved easily in his mind; those concerned with intimate human relations were rarely solved satisfactorily. In spite of the sentimentalizing often attributed to him, Lincoln's loyalties and abilities grew out of abstractions and ideas rather than from emotional attachments to human beings. The former he found stimulating and challenging; perhaps the harshness and uncertainty of frontier life had made the other difficult and dangerous for him to accept.

I   *The Letters to Mary Owens*

Three of Lincoln's letters to Miss Owens survive. Unlike his moot romance with Ann Rutledge, that with Miss Owens could hardly be considered romantic. Instead the three letters, of December 13, 1836, May 7, 1837, and August 16, 1837, are indicative not merely of Lincoln's uncertainty but of his inability to intellectualize emotion and his intuitive recognition that he could not. Mary Owens, educated and cultured, would be a suitable wife for an ambitious young lawyer—or so, perhaps, New Salem matchmakers and Lincoln himself thought. But the letters are those of a confused young man uncertain of himself or his motives and aware of an ambiguity in their relationship that he could not understand or resolve. Consequently, he was unable to make clear feelings that he could neither intellectualize nor ignore. None of the letters is that of a lover, and what understanding passed between them can only be deduced from them and from Miss Owens' comments thirty years later.

The first letter, written from Vandalia, is a combination of friendly information and inept innuendo. After a reference to the fact that he had been unwell and had nothing to write, he commented with disarming naïveté that "... the longer I can avoid the mortification of looking in the Post Office for your letter and not finding it, the better. You see I am mad about that *old letter* yet. I don't like verry well to risk you again. I'll try you once more any how" (I, 54). With that, he turned to state-house gossip and political partisanship before returning to the topic with which he had begun:

> You recollect I mentioned in the outset of this letter that I had been unwell. That is the fact, though I believe I am about well now; but that, with other things I can not account for, have conspired and have gotten my spirits so low, that I feel that I would rather be any place in the world than here. I really can not endure the thought of staying here ten weeks. Write back as soon as you get this, and if possible say something that will please me, for really I have not [been] pleased since I left you. This letter is so dry and [stupid] that I am ashamed to send it, with my pres[ent feel]ings I can not do any better. (I, 54–55)

This paragraph was not written by the self-confident young politician or by the forceful satirist of the previous summer; instead, it was by an uncertain young man unwilling and unable either to explore the nature of his own feelings or to trust or express them. Perhaps, too, behind the façade of that promising, able young politician who was seemingly eager to close in combat with the entire democracy, there was a secret fear of failure and rejection. The frontier upon which he was reared was neither emotionally nor sentimentally expressive in intimate personal relations; and, in the more sophisticated social circle into which he aspired to move, he found himself increasingly surrounded by the romantic sentimentality of the mainstream of nineteenth-century social behavior, a phenomenon that was to remain baffling to him but that absorbed the man in the Lincoln myth thirty years later. More important, however, the letter indicates that he was suffering, perhaps as a result of his uncertainty, from the melancholia that was to plague him at intervals for the rest of his life and that was ultimately to contribute to teaching him the personal compassion that frontier harshness so often obliterated in men.

The second letter, from Springfield, is less tortured and uncertain, but no less ambiguous. It is, he commented, the third letter he had attempted to write; the first was not serious enough; the other, too much so. He was lonesome and had not yet been to church because"... I am conscious I should not know how to behave myself" (I, 78). But these remarks were merely prefatory to what came close to a declaration and then moved quickly away from it, implying that an understanding existed, and yet unwilling to acknowledge it. The letter itself, like that of the following August, contains none of the unpracticed frankness of the first; it seems, in contrast, to be as carefully drawn as any of his legal documents of the period, placing all responsibility for the future course of their relationship upon Miss Owens. It is dominated by the seemingly humble frankness of his first political announcement, but there is no tangible evidence of his true feelings, just as there is no indication of continued intense melancholy:

> I am often thinking about what we said of your coming to live at Springfield. I am afraid you would not be satisfied. There is a great deal of flourishing about in carriages here, which it would be your doom to see without shareing in it. You would have to be poor without the means of hiding your poverty. Do you believe you could bear that patiently? Whatever woman may cast her lot with mine, should any ever do so, it is my intention to do all in my power to make her happy and contented; and there is nothing I can immagine, that would make me more unhappy than to fail in the effort. I know I should be much happier with you than the way I am, provided I saw no signs of discontent in you. What you have said to me may have been in jest, or I may have misunderstood it. If so, then let it be forgotten; if otherwise, I much wish you would think seriously before you decide. For my part I have already decided. What I have said I will most positively abide by, provided you wish it. My opinion is that you had better not do it. You have not been accustomed to hardship, and it may be more severe than you now immagine. I know you are capable of thinking clearly on any subject; and if you deliberate maturely upon this, before you decide, then I am willing to abide your decision. (I, 78)

There is no record of Miss Owens' reply, and Lincoln's dilemma continued its ambiguous course, making inevitable the misconstructions and controversies that continue to surround the relationship. But in this letter Lincoln was in command of himself; and, whatever his true feelings were, they are not apparent. A man of honor on one hand and a shrewd, practical political lawyer on the other, he presented both the dilemma and a carefully ambiguous solution to Miss Owens.

In the final letter, written from Springfield the following August, the ambiguity remained—one evidently to be resolved shortly thereafter by Miss Owens. But the ambiguity is less misleading; Lincoln, it appears, would prefer his freedom, but appearances may be deceptive. Nevertheless, melancholia and loneliness are gone; there is no hint of passion, but there is an air of eagerness to be frank that is reminiscent of his early political declarations. However, frankness itself, the basis of that earlier statement, is completely missing; instead, there is a deliberate evasiveness designed to permit Miss Owens to construe the letter as she will:

> You must know that I cannot see you, or think of you, with entire indifference, and yet it may be, that you, are mistaken in regard to what my real feelings towards you are. If I knew you were not, I should not trouble you with this letter ... I want in all cases to do right, and most particularly so, in all cases with women. I want, at this particular time, more than any thing else, to do right with you, and if I *knew* it would be doing right, as I rather suspect it would, to let you alone, I would do it ... If you feel yourself in any degree bound to me, I am now willing to release you, provided you wish it; while, on the other hand, I am willing, and even anxious to bind you faster, if I can be convinced that it will, in any considerable degree, add to your happiness ... Nothing would make me more miserable than to believe you miserable—nothing more happy, than to know you were so. (I, 94)

Two footnotes remain to this episode. The first is a gracious, sensitive letter from Miss Owens to William Herndon, written on May 22, 1866, in which she attributed her final decision to her belief that "... Mr. Lincoln was deficient in those little links which make up the chain of woman's happiness—at least it was so in my case. Not that I believed it proceeded from a lack of goodness of heart; but his training had been different from mine; hence there was not that congeniality which would otherwise have existed."[1] Perhaps the major link that Miss Owens found missing was sensitivity for the feelings of others; as she was aware, Lincoln still lacked human compassion, as the letters make clear, in spite of protests to the contrary by his biographers.

The other footnote to the episode is a letter from Lincoln to Mrs. Orville H. Browning, who, with her husband, was among

Lincoln's closest friends. This letter, written on April 1, 1838—perhaps, in view of its contents, a significant date—recounts, at Miss Owens' expense, the story of their abortive courtship. In the letter Lincoln was obviously attempting to be humorous, but the result is a coarse exaggeration of Miss Owens' personal defects, a grotesque kind of humor undoubtedly derived from innumerable frontier oral caricatures, but certainly not in keeping with Lincoln's asserted sincerity of intention toward her. In the letter he recalled that the engagement was the result of a promise made to her sister; and immediately after seeing Miss Owns again, for the first time in three years, he had regretted his rashness but was determined to be a gentleman and to honor his promise. But he was shocked:

> . . . I knew she was oversize, but now she appeared a fair match for Falstaff; I knew she was called an "old maid", and I felt no doubt of the truth of at least half of the appelation; but now, when I beheld her, I could not for my life avoid thinking of my mother, for her skin was too full of fat, to permit its contracting in to wrinkles; but from her want of teeth, weatherbeaten appearance in general, and from a kind of notion that ran in my head, that *nothing* could have commenced at the size of infancy, and reached her present bulk in less than thirtyfive or forty years; and, in short, I was not at all pleased with her. But what could I do? I had told her sister that I would take her for better or for worse; and I made a point of honor and conscience in all things, to stick to my word . . . (I, 118)

He did, of course, find good points: she had a handsome face and a ready wit. But he was determined to be free, with honor. He proposed; she refused; he proposed again, and again she refused. But then Lincoln turned the joke on himself, as it begins increasingly to appear that the letter itself was a joke; and he concluded in personal lamentation:

> My vanity was deeply wounded by the reflection, that I had so long been too stupid to discover her intentions, and at the same time never doubting that I understood them perfectly; and also, that she whom I had taught myself to believe no body else would have, had actually rejected me with all my fancied greatness; and to cap the whole, I then, for the first time, began to suspect that I was really a little in love with her. But let it all go. I'll try and outlive it. Others have been made fools of by the girls; but

this can never be with truth said of me. I most emphatically, in this instance, made a fool of myself. I have now come to the conclusion never again to think of marrying; and for this reason; I can never be satisfied with anyone who would be block-head enough to have me. (I, 119)

Lincoln's humorous intent is made clear in the final line as he asks Mrs. Browning to ". . . write me a long yarn about something to amuse me . . ." (I, 119), but the questions of taste and sensitivity remain. The letter was written for the eyes of Mrs. Browning alone; Miss Owens' name is never mentioned; the total effect is that of an exercise in satire; and perhaps the last lines are wry acknowledgment of rejection and inferiority.

But particularly important is the complete absence of any trace of insight into or empathy with Miss Owens' predicament in the letter. Perhaps, as Herndon and others insist, the affair with Miss Owens, and particularly the last letter, was a momentary lapse in an otherwise kind nature. But the letters suggest, rather, Lincoln's self-searching for compassion that he was unable to feel; and the recurring melancholy seems an intense awareness of that shortcoming. But it was a shortcoming not to be remedied until his nature was refined in the crucible of the war that was to come and that no amount of ambiguity or legalistic objectivity could evade or mitigate. As a young man, Lincoln knew that intense personal suffering existed; but he was unable or perhaps afraid to let himself feel it, as Miss Owens had evidently recognized.

The letters of this incident, as well as the later almost equally ambiguous and indecisive course of Lincoln's romance with Mary Todd, are part of his development as a master of poetic English prose. However, the letters do not foretell the brooding sensitivity of the artist, as has been asserted;[2] instead, they reveal a man who sought rational, logical answers in situations where none exist. In continuing to seek such answers, Lincoln was aware of the tragicomic implications of the search. But he was yet unable to accept and trust his emotions. Perhaps he laughed that he might not cry, but the letters indicate that he sought a rational, legalistic decisiveness which he knew intuitively could not exist in the circumstances. Consequently, he found it necessary to regard the affair as a joke, with the butt of it himself and Miss Owens.

The remarkable sensitivity of Lincoln's greatest speeches and writings had its origin in later, more intense experiences; the young lawyer of Springfield had not yet known the depth of human emotion that makes such utterances possible, and he knew that he had not. Four years later, however, he was to attempt, somewhat facetiously, to analyze rationally the similar emotional dilemma of his friend Josua Speed and, by implication, his own indecisive relationship with Mary Todd.

II *The First Statement on Slavery*

However uncertain and insensitive Lincoln was in his romance with Miss Owens, his decision to seek his future in the promising city of Springfield does suggest that, in determining the direction of his future, he could be objective and consistent. At the same time, as a surviving document of the period indicates, he maintained a rationally consistent attitude toward the institution of slavery and its legal position in the nation. Little factual data and much conjecture surround the origins of Lincoln's attitude toward both; perhaps his hatred of the institution was the result of his father's attitude and experiences in Kentucky, and certainly his recognition of its legality was the result of his study of the law. However, Lincoln's attitude was fixed as a young legislator; and a document signed by him and his colleague Dan Stone is the nucleus of what later became the legalistic argument that he debated with Stephen Douglas, the statement of his position in the Cooper Union speech, and the definition of issues in his inaugural address.

To Lincoln and Stone there was neither ambiguity nor uncertainty in the proper attitude toward slavery. The two protested, as a minority, a legalistic support of slavery accepted by the legislature in response to pleas from other states both North and South. To Lincoln at this time, both the issue and his attitude toward it were as clear as they would remain, even while the foundations of the country were shaken:

> Resolutions upon the subject of domestic slavery having passed both branches of the General Assembly at its present session, the undersigned hereby protest against the passage of the same.

They believe that the institution of slavery is founded on both injustice and bad policy; but that the promulgation of abolition doctrines tends rather to increase than to abate its evils.

They believe that the Congress of the United States has no power under the constitution, to interfere with the institution of slavery in the different States.

They believe that the Congress of the United States has the power, under the constitution, to abolish slavery in the District of Columbia; but that that power ought not to be exercised unless at the request of the people of said District.

The difference between these opinions and those contained in the said resolutions, is their reason for entering this protest. (I, 74–75)

This statement, legalistic and rational in thought and execution, not only is characteristic of the forthrightness which marked Lincoln's political statements of the period, but it indicates, too, the absence of radicalism or extremism in his attitude toward slavery as an institution or his suggestions for its abatement. Invariably the extreme hostility toward the institution by the Abolition movement was as illogical, irrational, and distasteful to Lincoln as the Southern extremist position; but to him the Abolitionists were guilty only of misguided zeal, whereas the South was morally wrong. In his distrust of both positions he sought a solution to the problem through a middle way as essentially conservative as it was rational. At the same time, in stating his position on this as a constitutional problem (based in the law to which he was dedicated), he did not equivocate or take refuge in ambiguity. Human problem though it was, to him it was nevertheless removed from human immediacy. Consequently, as a rational abstraction he believed that it, like the romance that he sought ineffectually to reduce to contractual terms, could be solved most easily and completely by the gradual limitation and eventual extinction of the institution through constitutionally sanctioned, rationally conceived means.

The dichotomy inherent in Lincoln's response to either a personal or a public crisis marks much of his thinking throughout the Springfield years until his election to the United States Congress in 1846 and his departure for Washington a year later. Not only did the melancholia recur at times of personal crisis, as in his courtship of Mary Todd between 1840 and their marriage on November 4, 1842, but during those same years his grasp of both the rational structure of the law and the practical nature of politics grew stronger. He was a rationalist and a realist by conviction, and his writing during these years is characterized by an increasingly lucid, often humorous incisiveness when it deals with politics and the law, while ambiguity, indecision, and an increasing evident sentimentality mark many of his personal writings and relationships.

While his public and professional statements and actions became mature quickly, his emotional life remained immature. The fusion of both in maturity, evident in the great utterances of the war years, was still far in the future, and Lincoln, as he moved into his thirties, was as fully developed intellectually as he was underdeveloped emotionally. Particularly evident is this dichotomy as it was revealed to John T. Stuart, his friend, mentor, law partner, and political colleague during the years of his courtship of the woman who was to become his wife.

III   *Love, Melancholia, and Politics*

With the exception of its outcome, Lincoln's courtship of Mary Todd closely paralleled his relationship with Mary Owens. Like her predecessor, Miss Todd was a Kentucky girl of good family, intelligence, a ready wit, and some education. Short and attractive, she was, according to the fashion of the day, pleasingly plump. While visiting the prominent Ninian Edwards, who had married her sister, Miss Todd was courted by a number of the young men of Springfield, among them Stephen A. Douglas and Abraham Lincoln, then rivals in love as they were to remain in politics. Folklore insists that she was determined to marry the man with the best chance of becoming President, and during 1840 she apparently chose Lincoln. Much debate centers over an allegedly scheduled wedding on January 1, 1841; Lincoln's failure to show up; and a subsequent long period of melancholy. Evidently a break between them did occur, but during the following months, including the day presumably scheduled for the wedding, Lincoln was reasonably faithful in his attendance in the legislature, in court, and in political affairs.

Nevertheless, his letters to Stuart, then in Congress, record his

torment. On January 20, 1841, after an absence of a week from
the legislature and much gossip and speculation among his
friends and rivals, he wrote a strained plea to Stuart that Dr.
Anson G. Henry be appointed to the postmastership of Springfield: "I have, within the last few days, been making a most
discreditable exhibition of myself in the way of hypochondriaism
and thereby got an impression that Dr. Henry is necessary to my
existence. Unless he gets that place, he leaves Springfield" (I,
228). In a desperate attempt to regain his balance, he concluded,
"Pardon me for not writing more; I have not sufficient composure
to write a long letter" (I, 228).

Three days later, in spite of having returned to his duties in
the legislature, the melancholia persisted; and, after attempting
to write a detailed political letter to Stuart, he returned again
to his fears and misery:

> For not giving you a general summary of news, you *must* par-
> don me; it is not in my power to do so. I am now the most mis-
> erable man living. If what I feel were equally distributed to the
> whole human family, there would not be one cheerful face on the
> earth. Whether I shall ever be better I can not tell; I awfully
> forbode I shall not. To remain as I am is impossible; I must die
> or be better, it appears to me. The matter you speak of on my
> account, you may attend to as you say, unless you shall hear of
> my condition forbidding it. I say this, because I fear I shall be
> unable to attend to any bussiness here, and a change of scene
> might help me. If I could be myself, I would rather remain at
> home with Judge Logan. I can write no more. Your friend, as
> ever— (I, 229–30)

At this point, Lincoln attempted to bury himself in his work,
and his melancholia evidently eased; but it remained a source
of speculation in Springfield and concern among his friends.
However, during the following weeks he took an active role in
the legislative debates over internal transportation improvements
and financing, and the search for a stable state banking and fiscal
system. As in the past, Lincoln's speeches and remarks on these
topics were forceful, rational, and legalistic; the compartmental-
izing of his personal and private, emotional and rational affairs
seems to have resumed its effectiveness. Withdrawn from society
—apparently in the effort to avoid meeting Miss Todd, for on
June 12 she wrote that Lincoln "... deems me unworthy of

notice, as I have not met *him* in the gay world for months . . ."³—
he felt his composure gradually return, and that summer he engaged in a sensational murder trial and took a trip to Kentucky,
both of which engrossed and excited him. Only briefly, however,
in an encounter with slavery on the steamboat, did he reveal an
attempt to understand and rationalize suffering; during those
months, his control, after the earlier upset, is remarkable.

Historical, biographical, and mythological speculation has
found this period of emotional upheaval fascinating; when not
discounted as inexplicable, it has been advanced as evidence of
Lincoln's deep capacity for emotional feeling; as evidence of
a sensitive, poetically brooding nature; and as foreshadowing
his mystic compassion for the Union and its people. Supporters
of the last view see in Lincoln's suffering at this time the source
of his ability to understand the hearts of others and to reach
them in the magnificent statements of sympathy, compassion,
and understanding that he was to make in the future.

But such explanations seek a simple cause-effect relationship
that ignores one important fact: only rarely and briefly, in all
of Lincoln's writing or speaking until after his election to the
Presidency and the outbreak of the war, is there evidence of the
merger of emotion and reason that characterizes those later documents. Nor, during that twenty years, is there evidence of his
learning to understand, control, and direct that emotion. Instead,
it was suppressed; its force was diverted in the pursuit of clarity
and order in objective legal exercises; and his personal relationships were often cool and distant, impersonal, or even humorous. Often they were also the result of conventional middle-class
personal ambition.

During 1841 and 1842 Lincoln regained his composure, and
the means by which he sought personal salvation during those
months were those that made possible his later reputation as a
man of moderation and intellectual understanding. At the same
time, he regained his ability to suppress and control his emotions;
and, as his melancholia eased, he returned to the confident, impersonal, ambitious state of his early years in New Salem, during
which he had put aside his family ties, his inherited convictions,
and his frontier loyalties. Once again he was determined to rise
on the crest of the wave that swept frontier Mid-America into
the mainstream of nineteenth-century civilization. By late 1842

he was once more on his way up, a part of the forces of change that were to be more far-reaching than anyone, including himself, could possibly anticipate.

IV *The Trailor Incident and the "Rebecca Letters"*

Two incidents of the early 1840's, the trial of William Trailor for the apparent murder of Archibald Fisher in June, 1841, and the publication and aftermath of the "Rebecca Letters" in the late summer of 1842, mark the resurgence of Lincoln's sense of humor. As it had been in the past, it is once more often broad, barbed, and insensitive—indicative perhaps of a search for a dramatic and funny means of denying the demanding, threatening, and tragic nature of life. During those years Lincoln's humor was rooted in an awareness of human frailty; and it served him as a weapon against others and as a shield to protect himself from the demands of emotion.

In the Trailor incident in which a man was arrested for murdering another who had simply disappeared, described in a letter from Lincoln to Joshua Speed on June 19, 1841, Lincoln had participated as a lawyer; but he had remained detached, and the resulting description is a fast-moving, detailed narrative that resembles a comedy of errors, misunderstandings, and misinterpretations—all of which Lincoln, with the seeming naïveté of a comic artist, exploited to the fullest. "It was," he concluded,

> amusing to scan and contemplate the countenances, and hear the remarks of those who had been actively engaged in the search for the [nonexistent] dead body. Some looked quizical, some melancholly, and some furiously angry. Porter, who had been very active, swore he always knew the man was not dead, and that *he* had not stirred an inch to hunt for him; Langford, who had taken the lead in cutting down Hickoxes mill dam, and wanted to hang Hickox for objecting, looked most awfully wo-begone; he seemed the "wictim of hunrequited haffection" as represented in the comic almanic we used to laugh over; and Hart . . . said it was too *damned* bad, to have so much trouble, and no hanging after all." (I, 257–58)

Lincoln minimized his role as defense attorney in favor of telling well a funny story; melancholia was not apparent; and the Lincoln who perhaps preferred the personal safety to be found in laughter and who certainly perceived the irony of the human predicament and enjoyed a good laugh was clearly in command. Humor, whether comic or satiric, was to be important in his career and his personal life during the 1840's.

The second incident, in the late summer of 1842, was equally a comedy of errors; but Lincoln was a participant rather than an observer. This was the incident surrounding the "Rebecca letters," a series of four satirical political letters that appeared in the *Sangamo Journal* during August and September. The first, a comparatively mild satirical personal attack upon James Shields, the Democratic auditor of state accounts, was published on August 19; its authorship is in doubt, as is that of the last two, which appeared on September 9. The author of the second, published on September 2, was Lincoln; and the series, or part of it, was apparently the result of a silly collusion among Lincoln, Mary Todd, with whom he had become reconciled, and her friend Julia Jayne.

In the second letter, Lincoln's frontier satirical wit, broad and yet pointed, unleashed an attack upon Shields's honesty, his intelligence, and his political legitimacy. In the letter "Aunt Becca," a backwoods farm woman, engendered and recorded the diatribes of "Jefferson," a Democrat who felt that Shields was such a liar that he must be a Whig. If not, Jefferson asserted, then he would become one himself. In conclusion, Rebecca begged that the editors set the electorate straight on the matter:

> And now Mr. Printer, will you be sure to let us know in your next paper whether this Shields is a whig or a democrat? I don't care about it for myself, for I know well enough how it is already, but I want to convince Jeff. It may do some good to let him, and others like him, know *who* and *what* these *officers* of *State* are. It may help to send the present hypocritical set to where they belong, and to fill the places they now disgrace with men who will do more work, for less pay, and take a fewer airs while they are doing it. It ain't sensible to think that the same men who get us into trouble will change their course; and yet its pretty plain, if some change for the better is not made, its not long that neither Peggy, or I, or any of us, will have a cow left to milk, or a calf's tail to wring. (I, 296–97)

Much of the letter is in the style of the popular semiliterate political satire that spread from the frontier, in the works of

Artemus Ward and David Ross Locke (Petroleum Vesuvius Nasby), to become a weapon in the political wars of the nineteenth century. Not only did Lincoln enjoy satire of this sort for the rest of his life, but he was to practice it again in Congress. Its basis is burlesque, much as was his description of the real search for the alleged body a year before; but behind the letter is a clear intent to make Shields ridiculous. The effort is so unrestrained that it borders on criminal libel, a cause for action with which Lincoln should have been familiar and of which he should have been wary. Nevertheless, as in Swift and in Lincoln's earlier letter to Robert Allen, Lincoln let the mask of Rebecca slip; and what might have been strong but ambiguous satire is revealed for what it is: a merciless personal as well as political attack upon Shields.

Shortly thereafter, as a result, the comedy threatened to become a tragedy before continuing its course. Shields challenged Lincoln to a duel so that he might receive satisfaction for unprovoked slander and abuse; Lincoln accepted, his seconds naming cavalry broadswords as the weapons, and the two parties slipped across the Mississippi River to avoid prosecution under the Illinois law against duelling. As the two waited to begin, Lincoln, sitting on a log, reached up with his sword to cut a twig from a tree far beyond Shields's reach. Apparently as a result of this display, the seconds conferred, a statement was drawn up in which Lincoln admitted writing the letter with no intent to defame Shields, and the matter was settled.

As the party returned to the Illinois shore, the comedy resumed. The crowd waiting at Alton saw what appeared to be a man, dreadfully wounded, on the deck of the boat. But the "wounded" man was a log covered with a red shirt; the duelers had a good laugh at the expense of the curiosity seekers; and Lincoln and Shields parted friends, to share mutually in editorial denunciation for having escaped the punishment due those who violated the laws. The duel, and the irrational romanticism that it represented, had for Lincoln become a joke, as he undoubtedly had intended from the beginning.

V The Rationale of Slavery and Love

If broad humor had during these months once more become

"... he ... removed to Springfield, and commenced the practice ..."

a major part of Lincoln's public presence and very often an extension of the reason that he sought to emphasize, in his personal affairs he rarely sought or found occasions at which to laugh; he had determined that reason alone would be sufficient. After his return to Illinois from the Kentucky visit in the summer of 1841, he described his reaction to an encounter with the slave trade on the steamboat to St. Louis. Particularly remarkable is the absence of any indignation at this intimate glimpse of an institution for which he had no sympathy; instead, he significantly noted its inhumanity, but he observed also that the Negroes rose above it as he sought for himself a rationale of unhappiness and suffering. His description of the sight was sharp but rational:

> By the way, a fine example was presented on board the boat for contemplating the effect of *condition* upon human happiness. A gentleman had purchased twelve negroes in different parts of Kentucky and was taking them to a farm in the South. They were chained six and six together. A small iron clevis was around the left wrist of each, and this fastened to the main chain by a shorter one at a convenient distance from, the others; so that the negroes were strung together precisely like so many fish upon a trot-line. In this condition they were being separated forever from the scenes of their childhood, their friends, their fathers and mothers, and brothers and sisters, and many of them, from their wives and children, and going into perpetual slavery where the lash of the master is proverbially more ruthless and unrelenting than any other where; and yet amid all these distressing circumstances, as we would think them, they were the most cheerful and apparently happy creatures on board. One, whose offence for which he had been sold was an over-fondness for his wife, played the fiddle almost continually; and the others danced, sung, cracked jokes, and played various games with cards from day to day. (I, 260)

The description, like that of the search for the nonexistent murder victim, is vivid and detailed; Lincoln saw and was able to recall and recount his observations graphically. But more important is the fact that here, as in his other remarks on slavery during these years, he was detached; and, although a great deal of potential for emotional expression exists in this account, there is none. Instead, in his last words on the incident, he tried to find meaning beyond it, a meaning that is rational rather than sentimental. Perhaps reminded of his almost intolerable emotional upset earlier that year, he saw in the incident a reminder of the durability of the human spirit and, significantly, he saw it in terms of the religious rationale that had been part of his childhood: "How true it is that 'God tempers the wind to the shorn lamb,' or in other words, that He renders the worst of human conditions tolerable, while He permits the best, to be nothing better than tolerable" (I, 260). With its emphasis on a religious faith, acceptance, and resignation seemingly incongruous in the life of the rational young prairie lawyer and legislator, this statement, transcending human suffering, anticipates the definition of an ultimate divine purpose that he was to present during the war, when he had begun to understand and to feel in himself the suffering in others. But at this time his approach to the suffering of others was objective and rational.

Like his attitude toward slavery, the resurgence of his political ambition is also an indication that the temporary personal depression of 1841 had run its course. In 1842, after a minor surge of support developed for his candidacy for the governorship, Lincoln felt that his eight years in the legislature had qualified him for higher office; and he determined to run for Congress. Refusing renomination for the legislature, he declared his ambition and began an active campaign, even opposing a number of his friends, for the nomination. Well aware of the inroads that the Whigs had made in what had so recently been the Jacksonian frontier, Lincoln knew that his ambition was not inordinate; but, at the district convention the following May, his friend John J. Hardin received the nomination. Much has been made of an alleged agreement among Hardin, Edward D. Baker, and Lincoln that would provide for rotating the nomination among them rather than risk the destruction of party chances. Some evidence supports the contention that the agreement was made, and Hardin, Baker, and Lincoln were nominated and elected in that order.

During the terms of his predecessors, Lincoln served faithfully as a political observer and fence-mender at home; and, in the Presidential election of 1844, he served as an elector, campaigning widely for Henry Clay. In the process he enhanced his own political reputation and acquaintanceship. Between 1842 and

"... he ... removed to Springfield, and commenced the practice ..."

his election to Congress in 1846, Lincoln became a state rather than local power in the Whig party; and it became evident that his ambitions, logically directed during those years, were not out of proportion to his ability or to reasonable expectations. Not only was his youthful madness over, but there seemed to be no likelihood of its recurrence.

In early 1842 Lincoln wrote a series of letters to Josua F. Speed, his closest friend of the period, in which he examined Speed's romantic uncertainty in rational detail; and, in doing so, Lincoln undoubtedly gained much insight into his own similar dilemma as the source of his melancholy. In the same letters it is evident that he was gaining increasing insight into the universality of human torment as well as what was frequently its source. Speed, like Lincoln, had been engaged in an uncertain, fearful romance that had resulted in doubts and melancholy; and Lincoln, in the attempt to assuage his friend's fear, sought to examine it logically and to dispel it. The effort failed temporarily in Speed's case, but it undoubtedly did much to ease and control Lincoln's own uncertainty. In January, 1842, with dry humor mixed freely with logical analysis and with tongue in cheek, he wrote the first letter, which Speed was to read for reassurance in moments of doubt:

Why I say it is reasonable that you will feel verry badly yet, is, because of *three special causes,* added to the *general one* which I shall mention.

The general cause is, that you are *naturaly of a nervous tempermanent,* and this I say from what I have seen of you personally, and what you have told me concerning your mother at various times, and concerning your brother William at the time his wife died.

The first special cause is, *your exposure to bad weather* on your journey, which my experience clearly proves to be verry severe on defective nerves.

The second is, *the absence of all business and conversation of friends,* which might divert your mind, and give it occasional rest from that *intensity* of thought, which will sometimes wear the sweetest idea thread-bare and turn it to the bitterness of death.

The third is, *the rapid and near approach of that crisis on which all your thoughts and feelings concentrate.*

If from all these causes you shall escape and go through triumphantly, without another "twinge of soul" I shall be most happily, but most egreriously deceived.

If, on the contrary, you shall, as I expect you will at some time, be agonized and distressed, let me, who have some reason to speak with judgement on such a subject, beseech you, to ascribe it to the causes I have mentioned; and not to some false and ruinous suggestion of the Devil. (I, 265)

From this wry effort at logical analysis Lincoln began to parody the technique of the courtroom. With equally subtle but pointed humor he began a cross-examination designed to establish the truth of Speed's attitude toward his fiancée and perhaps his own toward Miss Todd:

I know what the painful point with you is, at all times when you are unhappy. It is an apprehension that you do not love her as you should. What nonsense!—How came you to court her? Was it because you thought she desired it; and that you had given her reason to expect it? If it was for that, why did not the same reason make you court Ann Todd, and at least twenty others of whom you can think, & to whom it would apply with greater force than to *her*? Did you court her for her wealth? Why, you knew she had none. But you say you *reasoned* yourself *into* it. What do you mean by that? Was it not, that you found yourself unable to *reason* yourself *out* of it? Did you not think, and partly form the purpose, of courting her the first time you ever saw or heard of her? What had reason to do with it, at that early stage? . . .

Say candidly, were not those heavenly *black eyes* the whole basis of all your early *reasoning* on the subject? (I, 266)

In the course of the letter, Lincoln, with all the gentle irony of which he was capable, marshaled the evidence at the same time that he had a bit of fun with his friend. But, in spite of the humor, he was employing a technique that he had found effective in the courtrooms and political battles of central Illinois: a rationally developed examination of the situation stripped of all the overtones of emotion, and a ceaseless questioning designed to reveal the heart of the problem rather than supply answers. It was a technique that, more seriously applied, was to provide the basis for the great political debates with Stephen A. Douglas during the campaign of 1858 and in the Cooper Union in February, 1860. Later, too, he was effectively to apply this kind of gentle, teasing humor at times of domestic crisis in his marriage. But none of it was effective with his friend Speed.

Before the wedding, Speed's fiancée fell ill; and Speed, torn between fears for her death and fears that he might subconsciously wish it, wrote to Lincoln for help. Again Lincoln sought to reassure him in a letter devoid of humor that attempted to dispel the fears through logic and that pointed out the parallel situation in Lincoln's own experience. Significantly, too, Lincoln appended the comment that he had recovered from his own irrational fears:

> I would say more if I could; but it seems I have said enough. It really appears to me that you yourself ought to rejoice, and not sorrow, at this indubitable evidence of your undying affection for her. Why Speed, if you did not love her, although you might not wish her death, you would most calmly be resigned to it. Perhaps this point is no longer a question with you, and my pertenacious dwelling upon it, is a rude intrusion upon your feelings. If so, you must pardon me. You know the Hell I have suffered on that point, and how tender I am upon it. You know I do not mean wrong.
>
> I have been quite clear of hypo since you left—even better than I was along in the fall. (I, 268)

Apparently Speed's doubts were eased for a time; and Lincoln's next letter, which assumed that all was well, is a model of simple sincerity, combined with a little homily of practical advice: "I think if I were you, in case my mind were not exactly right, I would avoid being *idle*; I would immediately engage in some business or go to making preparations for it, which would be the same thing" (I, 269–70). Then, with the vividness of homely metaphor evident upon such occasions, he added: "I hope with tolerable confidence, that this letter is a plaster for a place that is no longer sore. God grant it may be so" (I, 270).

The plaster had evidently begun to work; in his next letter Speed confessed to being calmer although still haunted by frightening premonitions; and Lincoln turned to handwriting analysis and lecturing to discourage such foreboding, with continued references to his newly found understanding of his own state:

> I tell you, Speed, our *forebodings*, for which you and I are rather peculiar, are all the worst set of nonsense. I fancied, from

the time I received your letter of *saturday,* that the one of *wednesday* was never to come; and yet it *did* come, and what is more, it is perfectly clear, from both it's *tone* and *handwriting,* that you were much *happier,* or, if you think the term preferable, *less miserable,* when you wrote *it,* than when you wrote the last one before. You had so obviously improved, at the verry time I so much feared, you would have grown worse. (I, 280)

With a final warning on March 27 that Speed should expect his spirits to drop on occasion but to remember that inevitably they would revive, Lincoln's therapy for his friend came to an end; and perhaps in those months it had worked for himself also. In March, he cited his own unhappiness at Mary Todd's presumed unhappiness; but, by the fall of 1842, his personal affairs were in order. Although he confessed to Speed that he was too poor to visit Kentucky at the time, he was making plans for his own marriage to Miss Todd.

The previous October, Lincoln had made provision for a home for his father and stepmother by buying from them the family homestead, with life residency assured to them; and he also provided that his stepbrother, John D. Johnston, might buy it at no interest upon their deaths. In this transaction he apparently felt that he had discharged his obligation to his father and had given Johnston a motivation to work. But, although Lincoln's intimacy with Speed indicates that he was capable of a close relationship and that he had begun to understand Speed's predicament, Lincoln's relations with his father and his stepbrother remained distant. He had escaped from the aimless hard work of frontier farming; he had risen in the world; and he looked back only in times of necessity. The responsibility that he assumed in buying the farm was without sentiment or sympathy; it was an obligation and no more. Abraham Lincoln, pursuing his ambition, had neither time nor sympathy for those who failed to benefit from the transition to civilization. On later occasions, as when Johnston's helpless improvidence, so like Thomas Lincoln's, resulted in pleas for assistance, Lincoln responded, but his conviction was clear: logic and determination, rather than aimless surrender, were the impetus for success. But, during these years, Thomas Lincoln was silent; and one can only speculate on his attitude toward the son who was becoming the success that he was not.

On November 4, 1842, Lincoln and Mary Todd were married

in a quiet, sudden wedding among a group of friends and Todd relatives. Like the courtship, the wedding and the course of the marriage have been the subject of speculation; but Lincoln remained silent about both his attitude and reaction. A month before, however, he wrote to Speed, who was now avowedly happy: " 'Are you now, in *feeling* as well as in *judgement,* glad you are married as you are?' From any body but me, this would be an impudent question not to be tolerated; but I know you will pardon it in me. Please answer it quickly as I feel impatient to know" (I, 303). Contrary to Herndon's assertions, there is no evidence to indicate anything other than that Lincoln, the reluctant suitor, had at last reconciled himself to marriage, although there is nothing to suggest a grand passion on his part. Nor is there evidence of a resurgence of despair. Lincoln's political and legal activity continued unabated; he took his bride to board at the Globe Tavern, and a week after the ceremony he laconically wrote to Samuel Marshall that there was "Nothing new here, except my marrying, which to me is matter of profound wonder" (I, 305). Uncertainty gone, Lincoln's course was mapped out.

CHAPTER *4*

"... he was elected to the lower House of Congress, and served one term only ..."

BETWEEN his marriage and his fortieth birthday in 1849 Lincoln established a home and fathered two sons, but his interest during those years focused upon politics, especially upon his brief Congressional career, between December, 1847, and March, 1849, and upon the rapidly accelerating sectional crisis stirring the country. His fiscal policy as a Whig activist in Illinois and in Congress remained conservative, his tariff support coming unaltered from Henry Clay; but, in his attitude toward geographical expansion carrying with it the potential expansion of slavery, he grew increasingly radical, his declarations more forceful, and the rhetorical techniques upon which he depended more polished and effective. At the same time, he saw his Whig party go into the decline from which it never recovered; and at forty, apparently doomed by his allegiance to a lost cause, he returned to Springfield, convinced that he would have to find his success in the practice of law.

But these years were important in the development of his thinking and his ability to speak, to write, and to convince. By forty, however, he had not expanded the potential for feeling that was made evident in his friendship with Speed. It appears that he continued to feel the lack of sentiment in his own nature, and in verses, written in 1846, the result of a visit to his boyhood home in Indiana, he attempted to express conventionally nostalgic sentiments.

For the five years between his marriage and his departure for Washington, practical politics occupied most of his attention, with his law practice the means by which he supported his growing family. The firm of Logan and Lincoln enjoyed a substantial but modest practice, but the sharpness of inter- and intraparty warfare, including a determination to hold onto his prospects for election to Congress, was the most compelling aspect of his life. In the election of 1844, Lincoln, in support of Henry Clay, declared that the annexation of Texas was "inexpediant" and that John Tyler, the nominal Whig then in the White House, had been ill-advised in setting forth his terms for annexation. During the fall campaign he spoke widely, emphasizing the desirability of the protective tariff, the cornerstone of the Whig platform under Clay. In his retrospective analysis of the Whig failure, he saw the symptoms of what was to destroy the party and eventually to rend the country; but he had no idea of either the extent of the malady or the means of finding a cure:

> If the whig abolitionists of New York had voted with us last fall, Mr. Clay would now be president, whig principles in the ascendent, and Texas not annexed; whereas by the division, all that either had at stake in the contest, was lost . . . What was their process of reasoning, I can only judge from what a single one of them told me. It was this: "We are not to do *evil* that *good* may come." This general, proposition is doubtless correct; but did it apply? If by your votes you could have prevented the extention, &c. of slavery, would it not have been *good* and not *evil* so to have used your votes, even though it involved the casting of them for a slaveholder. By the *fruit* the tree is to be known. An *evil* tree can not bring forth *good* fruit. If the fruit of electing Mr. Clay would have been to prevent the extension of slavery, could the act of electing have been *evil?* (I, 347)

But Lincoln admitted that he had been lukewarm in his opposition to annexing Texas; to him it would have meant no real extension of slavery, because there were already slaves in the Republic of Texas and further movement into the area would simply mean fewer in the older slave states. The political implications, especially the resulting increased power of the slave bloc in government, seem to have eluded him. Consequently, this post-election search for the cause of defeat was not, to Lincoln, a matter of a choice between good and evil, but a rational attempt to define the origin of intraparty dissent, with the hope of alleviating such strife in the future. Lincoln was not searching for answers to the growing dilemma of slavery at this time; he was, in 1845, seeking a platform upon which all good Whigs could stand, just as he was to attempt to do the same thing for the Republican party in his speech at the Cooper Union in the late winter of 1860.

However much Lincoln attempted to interpret good and evil in regard to the slavery issue in terms of their relation to Whig political fortunes at this time, his personal position was clear; and it was to remain the same until military necessity and political expediency in the late summer of 1862 dictated a change:

> I hold it to be a paramount duty of us in the free states, due to the Union of the states, and perhaps to liberty itself (paradox though it may seem) to let the slavery of the other states alone; while, on the other hand, I hold it to be equally clear, that we should never knowingly lend ourselves directly or indirectly, to prevent that slavery from dying a natural death—to find new places for it to live in, when it can no longer exist in the old. Of course I am not now considering what would be our duty, in cases of insurrection among the slaves. (I, 348)

In noting this paradox, Lincoln intuitively recognized the basic ambiguity inherent in the American ideal of the eighteenth century and embodied in the debate between the two sections of the country and the factions within both major parties. This ambiguity stemmed from conflicting and overlapping definitions of natural rights as America professed its belief in the sanctity of liberty and property at the same time, failing to see that they were not synonymous. Within the context of the Constitution there was no satisfactory solution to the paradox unless in a time of crisis a solution one way or the other might be forced; and in 1845 Lincoln, with his grasp of the logical illogicality inherent in the legal status of the institution, knew it. But neither he nor any of his contemporaries foresaw at the time either the ramifications of the problem or the ultimate crisis that would resolve it.

Nevertheless, this document illustrates the clearness with which Lincoln examined complex political and social problems in his capacity as a politically active private citizen during the 1840's, and it demonstrates his ability to reduce them to their simplest elements in prose that deliberately avoided both subtlety and ambiguity. However, the fact that he was beginning to seek other than pragmatic uses for the words which he used so clearly is evident from his attempts at verse writing and at writing descriptive prose during 1846. He had visited his

boyhood home territory in Indiana on a speaking tour during
the campaign of 1844; and, perhaps as respite from his campaign
for Congress, he attempted to make poetry of the memories
resurrected by the visit. Of the efforts, three poems, one of them
in two versions, survive, as does his factual essay of the same
period, based on the Trailor murder case of 1841.

I The Verses of 1846

All three of the 1846 poems are sentimental ballads, each of
them a nostalgic evocation of the past in the Romantic tradition
of the safe Victorian poets whose works were found in every
American home aspiring to gentility. This verse tradition was
imitated in country newspapers throughout America west of the
Appalachians and east of the Mississippi during the nineteenth
century. Although Lincoln's verse was in the vein satirized by
Mark Twain in *Huckleberry Finn*, Lincoln was neither an
Emmaline Grangerford; nor, thanks to his memories of the grim
nature of his childhood environment and occasional flashes of
wry humor, did he become, like Julia A. Moore, a sweet singer
of Indiana.

But to see in the weak, unskilled, and theatrical verse that he
produced at this time a foreshadowing of the prose poems at
Gettysburg, as some critics have unfortunately done, is to stretch
a coincidental authorship to an unacceptable extent; they are
conventional bad poems. Lincoln had worked at revising the
verses and had allowed Andrew Johnston to publish them anonymously, but he knew that he was no poet in the conventional
sense. Of William Knox's "Mortality" he wrote, "I would give all
I am worth, and go in debt, to be able to write so fine a piece
as I think that is" (I, 378); and in respect to his own verse he
was under no illusions. But he was not ashamed of his venture
into verse, as he recounted its inception to Johnston:

> In the fall of 1844, thinking I might aid some to carry the
> State of Indiana for Mr. Clay, I went into the neighborhood in
> that State in which I was raised, where my mother and only
> sister were buried, and from which I had been absent about fif-
> teen years. That part of the country is, within itself, as unpoetical
> as any spot of the earth; but still, seeing it and its objects and

inhabitants aroused feelings in me which were certainly poetry; though whether my expression of those feelings is poetry is quite another question. (I, 378)

In seeking to express the depth of those feelings in the conventional jingle-like ballad form that he chose, Lincoln did not write the poetry that he might have on that occasion and that he was to do on equally or more stirring occasions in the future. The regularity of rhyme and rhythm inevitably distorted and cheapened the emotions that he felt. But his effort at creative expression at this time is important, not for its accomplishment but for its intent. Emotion, Lincoln was beginning to learn, is neither shameful nor to be feared, nor is it to be rejected by reason. Instead, it can elevate man to a new awareness, a new insight into himself and the human experience.

The verses as they survive in fragments fall naturally into three parts, two of them cantos of what was a projected or actual four-canto work, and the third a rousing narrative that may have been the third of the projected four cantos.[1] Cantos one and two, revised by Lincoln in the spring and summer of 1846, describe the nostalgic impact of the return to boyhood scenes and the sense of loss, of death, of emptiness that those scenes engendered. The first is a general recollection of emotion, and the second explores in detail the microcosmic tragedy of a mad boy before pondering again on the unknowable logic of death. He began by examining the memory of his childhood emotions as he looked about the scene:

> My childhood's home I see again,
>   And sadden with the view;
> And still, as memory crowds my brain,
>   There's pleasure in it too.
>
> O Memory! thou midway world
>   'Twixt earth and paradise,
> Where things decayed and loved ones lost
>   In dreamy shadows rise,
>
> And, freed from all that's earthly vile,
>   Seem hallowed, pure and bright,
> Like scenes in some enchanted isle
>   All bathed in liquid light.

As dusky mountains please the eye
    When twilight chases day;
As bugle-notes that, passing by,
    In distance die away;

As, leaving some grand waterfall,
    We, lingering, list its roar—
So memory will hallow all
    We've known, but know no more.

Near twenty years have passed away
    Since here I bid farewell
To woods and fields, and scenes of play,
    And playmates loved so well.

Where many were, but few remain
    Of old familiar things;
But seeing them, to mind again
    The lost and absent brings.

The friends I left that parting day,
    How changed, as time has sped!
Young childhood grown, strong manhood gray,
    And half of all are dead.

I hear the loved survivors tell
    How naught from death could save,
Till every sound appears a knell
    And every spot a grave.

I range the fields with pensive tread,
    And pace the hollow rooms,
And, feel (companion of the dead)
    I'm living in the tombs. (I, 378–79)

Like much of the graveyard poetry of the eighteenth century,
the period that provided the model and inspiration for Lincoln's
adherence to reason, this introductory canto is bathed in Romantic pathos, platitudes, and a morbid awareness of the omnipresence of death, a commonplace on the frontier as in the lives
of the folk in Thomas Gray's famous churchyard. The sentiments
are genuine, as Lincoln commented in his accompanying letter
to Johnston; but the result is not. Instead, he was forced into
stereotyped diction by the narrow regularity of the form. The
clichés are only occasionally redeemed by an original image.

But the unbroken tone of mournful regret, the regularity of rhythm and rhyme, make the poem expressive neither of Lincoln nor of the harsh impact of a past softened by time. Instead, its nostalgia is conventionally sentimental.

In the second canto, in spite of close adherence to the conventions of the first, Lincoln moved toward mythmaking in the frontier tradition as he dealt with a story that had its counterpart in almost every area of the mid-American frontier, many of which have become part of the Midwestern literary heritage. This is the story of Mathew Gentry, a former schoolmate of Lincoln's who had gone violently mad and then became harmlessly insane. In moving from the pensive to the descriptive, Lincoln's verse takes on an active movement and vitality at odds with the first canto; and the subject permits a blunt diction taken from life. Finally, however, the verse bogs down in the same pensive wonder that marked the first. Like the other canto, this verse retains its grimness from first to last; but the violence has the force of reality:

> But here's an object more of dread
> Than ought the grave contains—
> A human form with reason fled,
> While wretched life remains.
>
> Poor Mathew! Once of genius bright,
> A fortune-favored child—
> Now locked for aye, in mental night,
> A haggard mad-man wild.
>
> Poor Mathew! I have n'er forgot,
> When first, with maddened will,
> Yourself you maimed, your father fought,
> And mother strove to kill;
>
> When terror spread, and neighbors ran,
> Your dange'rous strength to bind;
> And soon, a howling crazy man
> Your limbs were fast confined.
>
> How then you strove and shrieked aloud,
> Your bones and sinews bared;
> And fiendish on the gazing crowd,
> With burning eyeballs glared—

> And begged, and swore, and wept, and prayed
>   With maniac laughter joined—
> How fearful were those signs displayed
>   By pangs that killed thy mind!
>
> And when at length, tho' drear and long,
>   Time soothed thy fiercer woes,
> How plaintively thy mournful song
>   Upon the still night rose.
>
> I've heard it oft, as if I dreamed,
>   Far distant, sweet and lone—
> The funeral dirge, it ever seemed
>   Of reason dead and gone.
>
> To drink its strains, I've stole away,
>   All stealthily and still,
> Ere yet the rising God of day
>   Had streaked the Eastern hill.
>
> Air held his breath; trees, with the spell,
>   Seemed sorrowing angels round,
> Whose swelling tears in dew-drops fell
>   Upon the listening ground.
>
> But this is past; and naught remains,
>   That raised thee o'er the brute.
> Thy piercing shrieks, and soothing strains,
>   Are like, forever mute.
>
> Now fare thee well—more thou the *cause,*
>   Than *subject* now of woe.
> All mental pangs, by time's kind laws,
>   Has lost the power to know.
>
> O death! Thou awe-inspiring prince,
>   That keepst the world in fear;
> Why doest thou tear more blest ones hence,
>   And leave him ling'gring here? (I, 385–86)

Certainly more original and vivid than the first canto, this one is at the same time less unified in statement as Lincoln found himself restricted by a form demanding a more conventional subject than the violence of insanity. Consequently, in contrast to the first, distortions abound, the verse is less polished, and irregularities recur. But much of the diction is startlingly fresh, with the vivid Anglo-Saxon force of the frontier; and mournful monotony is allayed by primitive vitality.

The third verse, perhaps intended as the third canto, carries on the original strain of "Poor Mathew," but the mournful nostalgia is gone; and the subject is a lively recounting of a bear hunt, its intensity relieved by wry humor. Less strained in its structure, it is less pretentious and less polished; and at its core is an unfeeling, unfelt violence at home in its setting. Even the infrequent nostalgic notes take on the atmosphere of violence in which there is neither strain nor falsity. As Lincoln describes it, the bear hunt *is:*

> A wild-bear chace, didst never see?
> Then hast thou lived in vain.
> Thy richest bump of glorious glee,
> Lies desert in thy brain.
>
> When first my father settled here,
> 'Twas then the frontier line:
> The panther's scream, filled night with fear
> And bears preyed on the swine.
>
> But wo for Bruin's short lived fun,
> When rose the squealing cry;
> Now man and horse, with dog and gun,
> For vengeance, at him fly.
>
> A sound of danger strikes his ear;
> He gives the breeze a snuff:
> Away he bounds, with little fear,
> And seeks the tangled *rough.* (I, 386–87)

From this point it is a merry, confused chase as the hue and cry bring on the dogs and the "merry *corps*"; then, cornered at bay, worn from the chase, the bear stands to fight and die:

> And furious now, the dogs he tears,
> And crushes in his ire.
> Wheels right and left, and upward rears,
> With eyes of burning fire.
>
> But leaden death is at his heart,
> Vain all the strength he plies.
> And, spouting blood from every part,
> He reels, and sinks, and dies. (I, 388)

"...he was elected to the lower house of Congress,
and served one term only..."

But at this moment there is no questioning or pondering; death, sudden and bloody, is a necessary fact for the bear; and Lincoln wastes no time on false sentiment. Instead, in keeping with the lusty tradition of which the hunt is a part, he portrays the comedy of the confusion and the universality of its human aftermath:

> And now a dinsome clamor rose,
>   'Bout who should have his skin;
> Who first draws blood, each hunter knows,
>   This prize must always win.

> But who did this, and how to trace
>   What's true from what's a lie,
> Like lawyers, in a murder case
>   They stoutly *argufy*. (I, 388)

Sentiment is gone, replaced by a gentle contempt devoid of the emotion in the early poems. The human comedy, in contrast to the dumb courage of the bear, is ludicrous. And that ultimate irony is emphasized in the last lines, when a dog who had hung back comes forward to attack the corpse. Emulating his human companions, he parodies their nonsense, giving Lincoln additional opportunity for wry, pointed comment as the dog moves to the attack,

> And swells as if his skin would tear,
>   And growls and shakes again;
> And swears, as plain as dog can swear,
>   That he has won the skin.

> Conceited whelp! we laugh at thee—
>   Nor mind, that not a few
> Of pompous, two-legged dogs there be,
>   Conceited quite as you. (I, 389)

No poet in the conventional sense, Lincoln's eye and ear at this time were for the real, as was his innate sense of language, forceful, clear, simple, and active. In letting form control idea in the earlier verse, sentiment was distorted to unreality; and in this verse, it impedes action. But the mock-heroic satire of this verse, together with the keen sense of ironic comedy and the shrewd insight into pompous nonsense, give "The Bear Hunt" a verisimilitude that transcends its form by using its story as well as its form as a comic device. The rude, forceful combination produces a rough humor in which the hunt is like the ridiculous paradox of life, and violence is only a passing shadow to be ignored in the spirit of fun. Lincoln focuses not on tragedy but on foolishness, the sympathy for animals so much a part of the Lincoln myth is strangely absent, and the stark comedy of frontier life and humor prevails.

In spite of the obvious weaknesses in this brief collection of verse, it is evident that Lincoln—who largely continued to regard words pragmatically although he read widely in imaginative verse—was beginning to see language as more than a precision instrument. During this respite from preparing legislative documents, bills, and speeches, he attempted to explore the esthetic and emotional use of language, and the result suggests that, had he pursued it, he might have become one of the many minor poets who achieved local and regional fame as the stabilizing Midwest sought to compensate for the crudeness of its recent past. Fortunately, Lincoln did not join this movement; equally fortunate was his increasing awareness of the emotional and aesthetic poetential of words. That awareness, purged of its naïve adherence to the conventional demands of popular verse, was to lead to a personal restraint in the poetically provocative prose of the future. But the emotional maturity and simplicity of those later statements were not yet apparent.

II   *The Essay on the Trailor Case*

During 1846 Lincoln also turned his hand to narrative reporting, publishing anonymously in the Quincy *Whig* on April 15 an account of the Trailor murder case of five years before. Straightforward and factual, the story emphasizes the qualities of coincidence and circumstance in bringing about charges of murder when none had been committed, and the accidental discovery of the truth. In the article, as in the verses on Mathew Gentry and the bear hunt, Lincoln was dealing with the raw material of folklore. Lincoln, like others who grew up on the frontier, seems to have been aware of the importance of preserving these tales. He delighted in telling them, as much for his readers' and listeners' edification as for his own pleasure; and, as he participated in the Trailor case, he had been impressed by the implications it contained for the often conflicting qualities of justice and legality. In his essay he gave attention to the details of the case and then suggested the course of speculation such implications made necessary:

> It is not the object of the writer of this, to enter into the many curious speculations that might be indulged upon the facts of this narrative; yet he can scarcely forbear a remark upon what would, almost certainly have been the fate of William and Archibald [Trailor], had Fisher not been found alive. It seems he had wandered away in mental derangement, and, had he died in this condition, and his body been found in the vicinity, it is difficult to conceive what could have saved the Trailors from the consequence of having murdered him. Or, if he had died, and his body never found, the case against them, would have been quite as bad, for, although it is a principle of law that a conviction for murder shall not be had, unless the body of the deceased be discovered, it is to be remembered that Henry [Trailor] testified he saw Fisher's dead body. (I, 376)

Although Lincoln refrained from pushing the speculations beyond this point, the editor of the *Whig* did so, a fact that suggests possible collusion between the two. The editor saw in it implications that "... commend it to the attention of those at present engaged in discussing reforms in criminal jurisprudence, and the abolition of capital punishment."[2] Although Lincoln's friends were well aware of his authorship of the article, there is no recorded response to those editorial comments, but his continued preoccupation with the case is perhaps indicative of a tacit agreement and a political trial balloon.

In this article, as in the verses, factual details abound, even to the point of impeding the flow of the narrative; but, in spite of their bulk and occasional lapses into the clichés of nineteenth-century journalism, the story moves quickly, taking on elements of the macabre and ludicrous as graves are opened, dams destroyed, and finally the victim is brought alive into the courtroom. Evident in the account is a sense of dramatic suspense and of tragicomic human frailty not evident in Lincoln's political or personal writing during those years and that he did not exploit until the years of crisis and war in the future.

Lincoln's brief career as an imaginative writer ended as suddenly as it had begun when, in the fall of 1846, he became once more preoccupied with politics. He had been elected to Congress on August 3, 1846, and was to take his seat in December, 1847; in the intervening months he spent much of his time working on his Whig political fences and arranging his thoughts, particularly on the crucial tariff issue. At the same time Lincoln and his new law partner William Herndon were busy in the constant round of litigation indicative of a successful rural law practice, and there was no more time for the recollection and introspection that engendered his brief literary interlude.

The election of 1846 was critical for both Lincoln and the nation. James Polk, a Tennessee Jacksonian Democrat, had been narrowly elected to the Presidency under Jackson's sponsorship in 1844, and his function as he and Jackson saw it was to reunite a party that had begun to reflect the increasing stresses of sectionalism in the country. Consequently, unlike Martin Van Buren, Polk strongly advocated the Southern and Western-favored annexation of Texas, he sought a tariff reduction, and he demanded the re-establishment of an independent treasury system. Upon taking office he moved rapidly and strongly toward achieving those goals, all of them denounced by Henry Clay and his Whig followers, Lincoln among them.

III *The Religious Statement of 1846*

In the Congressional election, with the Mexican War intensifying and increased agitation over slavery becoming more vocal, Lincoln's opponent was Peter Cartwright, a staunch Jacksonian who had moved West with the frontier as a Methodist circuit rider. The campaign issued around personalities as well as party principles. Even religion became an issue as Cartwright, defender as well as preacher of staunch frontier fundamentalism, questioned Lincoln's orthodoxy. The result was Lincoln's frankest public statement on the nature of his beliefs, a document as significant for its omissions as for its assertions. Neither a church member nor an orthodox believer, Lincoln, in the handbill answering Cartwright's charges, placed his emphasis upon what he did not do rather than upon his own beliefs:

> That I am not a member of any Christian Church is true; but I have never denied the truth of the Scriptures; and I have never spoken with intentional disrespect of religion in general,

or of any denomination of Christians in particular. It is true that
in early life I was inclined to believe in what I understand is
called the "Doctrine of Necessity"—that is, that the human mind
is impelled to action, or held in rest by some power, over which
the human mind itself has no control; and I have sometimes
(with one, two or three, but never publically) tried to maintain
this opinion in argument. (I, 382)

Neither belief nor lack of it is evident in the letter except by
implication. Although Lincoln was reluctant to make such an
intimate matter the subject of a stump debate, he went on to the
attack, stating his concept of the proper role of religion in political candidacy; and then he denounced those whose accusations
had raised the issue:

I do not think I could myself, be brought to support a man
for office, whom I knew to be an open enemy of, and scoffer at,
religion. Leaving the higher matter of eternal consequences, between him and his Maker. I still do not think any man has the
right thus to insult the feelings, and injure the morals, of the
community in which he may live. If, then, I was guilty of such
conduct, I should blame no man who should condemn me for it;
but I do blame those, whoever they may be, who falsely put such
a charge in circulation against me. (I, 382)

The issue was apparently resolved by this statement, certainly
both political and conventional enough in nature; and on August
3 Lincoln was elected congressman from the Seventh Illinois
District by the largest majority received by a candidate in that
district up to that time. Although voting the straight Whig ticket
otherwise, he had cast his congressional ballot for Cartwright.
Then he proceeded with the political duties of a congressman-
elect.

But the question of Lincoln's religious beliefs was not resolved
by this statement, nor has it been resolved yet. As this document
states, he rejected both the literalness and the emotionalism of
revivalism when he rejected his background upon reaching his
maturity, and he seems to have evolved through his wide reading, particularly in the eighteenth century, a personal Deism
typical of the rational, inquiring mind. But he never escaped the
impact of the fundamental Christianity of his formative years,
and he was to return in spirit rather than practice to that faith,

particularly in the wisdom and justice of a personal God, in the years that were to come. Then the rationality of Deism no longer sufficed to explain or justify to him the surge of overwhelming, often anti-rational human emotion that is civil war.

The debate over the Mexican War continued while Lincoln prepared to go to Washington. His friend and predecessor, John J. Hardin, a volunteer, was killed at the battle of Buena Vista in Mexico; and Lincoln's opposition to America's first imperialist adventure intensified, as did that of his mentor, Henry Clay. On November 25, 1847, when the Lincolns started for Washington, Lincoln was determined to act as a decorous first-term congressman by refraining from participating in the intense partisan debate over the nature of and responsibility for the war. He found a place in Mrs. Sprigg's "boarding club" on Capitol Hill, took part in the organization of the slim Whig majority, and prepared to support the troops in the field while refraining from comment on the war. He did, however, plan to participate vigorously in the opposition to Polk's tariff program, and he had prepared notes to serve as the basis of speeches.

IV The "Spot Resolutions"

His weapon in attacking the lowered tariff was to be pure logic, as the notes reveal, a logic to be irrefutably and unanswerably phrased in a series of questions that demanded answers impossible to give except on Lincoln's own terms. This technique was the one that he had employed successfully on the stump, in the courtroom, and in the legislature; and he expected it to be as effective in Congress on the tariff issue. But, in his first major appearance on the Congressional floor, Lincoln forgot his earlier determination to refrain from debate on the war; instead, he used his questioning technique to attack the war, seeking to destroy Polk's position by disclosing that its aggressive outbreak was shoddy, dishonest, and deceitful. This initial speech, on December 22, was what became known as the "Spot Resolutions"; in it Lincoln demanded answers to questions that the official position refused to acknowledge existed. But Polk had requested Congressional acknowledgment that the war was just; and Lincoln, provoked by what he saw on Polk's arrogance, turned to the attack:

*"... he was elected to the lower house of Congress,
and served one term only ..."*

Whereas the President of the United States, in his message of
May 11th. 1846, has declared that "The Mexican Government
not only refused to receive him" (the envoy of the U.S.) "or
listen to his propositions, but, after a long series of menaces,
have at last invaded *our territory,* and shed the blood of our fellow *citizens on our own soil."*

And again, in his message of December 8, 1846 that "We
had ample cause of war against Mexico, long before the break-
ing out of hostilities. But even then we forebore to take redress
into our own hands, until Mexico herself became the agressor by
invading *our soil* in hostile array, and shedding the blood of our
citizens."

And yet again, in his message of December 7–1847 that "The
Mexican government refused even to hear the terms of adjust-
ment which he" (our minister of peace) "was authorized to propose; and finally, under wholly unjustifiable pretexts, involved
the two countries in war, by invading the territory of the State
of Texas, and shedding the blood of our *citizens* on *our own soil."*

And whereas this House desires to obtain a full knowledge of
all the facts which go to establish whether the particular spot of
soil on which the blood of our *citizens* was so shed, was, or was
not, our *own* soil, at that time; therefore

Resolved by the House of Representatives, that the President
of the United States be respectfully requested to inform this
House—

First: Whether the spot of soil on which the blood of our
citizens was shed, as in his messages declared, was, or was not,
within the territories of Spain, at least from the treaty of 1819
until the Mexican revolution.

Second: Whether that spot is, or is not, within the territory
which was wrested from Spain, by the Mexican revolution.

Third: Whether that spot is, or is not, within a settlement of
people, which settlement is, or is not, isolated from any and all
other settlements, by the Gulf of Mexico, and the Rio Grande,
on the South and West, and by wide uninhabited regions on the
North and East.

Fifth: Whether the *People* of that settlement, or a *majority*
of them, or *any* of them, had ever, previous to the bloodshed,
mentioned in his messages, submitted themselves to the govern-

ment or laws of Texas, or of the United States, by *consent,* or by *compulsion,* either by accepting office, or voting at elections, or paying taxes, or serving on juries, or having process served upon them, or in *any other way.*

Sixth: Whether the People of that settlement, did, or did not, flee from the approach of the United States Army, leaving unprotected their homes and their growing crops, *before* the blood was shed, as in his messages stated; and whether the first blood so shed, was, or was not shed, within the *inclosure* of the People, or of some of them, who had thus fled from it.

Seventh: Whether our *citizens,* whose blood was shed, as in his message declared, were, or were not, at that time, *armed* officers, and *soldiers,* sent into that settlement, by the military order of the President through the Secretary of War—and

Eighth: Whether the military force of the United States, including those *citizens,* was, or was not, so sent into that settlement, after Genl. Taylor had, more than once, intimated to the War Department that, in his opinion, no such movement was necessary to the defense or protection of Texas. (I, 420–22)

This speech was designed to destroy the position of the administration on the justification of the war; but the administration, with forces vastly superior to those of the Mexican army in Mexico or of Lincoln in Congress, did not deign to answer directly. Instead, the resolutions were tabled, and both the war and Lincoln's opposition to it continued. On January 3, 1848, he voted for the Whig-sponsored Ashmun amendment to the resolution commending General Taylor, whom Lincoln was supporting as a Whig Presidential candidate, for his victory at Buena Vista. The amendment, noting that the war was unnecessarily and unconstitutionally begun by Polk, was passed by the small Whig majority.

Shortly after his charges, using the techniques that had been successful in Illinois but unsuccessful in Congress except in providing support for the Whig position on the war, Lincoln began to become aware of an alarm in Congress and in his home congressional district over the unrestrained vigor of his attack. But before he attempted to justify his position, he had, on January 12, reiterated many of the same questions included in the "Spot Resolutions." The speech gave the answers Lincoln had demanded of the administration, emphasizing the dubious legality

". . . he was elected to the lower house of Congress, and served one term only . . ."

of the American claim to that "spot." But Lincoln's final demand in this speech was moral and emotional rather than rational or legal; President Polk was, he said, ". . . a bewildered, confounded, and miserably perplexed man. God grant he may be able to show, there is not something about his conscience, more painful than all his mental perplexity" (I, 441–42).

On February 1 Lincoln began a series of letters to Herndon and others in his congressional district who expressed an increasing dismay over Lincoln's attacks on the President and the war and particularly over his vote for the Ashmun amendment. In his defense he did not seek to evade the issue but to explain it by supporting his reasons with the facts as he saw them. The debate was, he said, a matter of truth or falsity, and he could neither evade nor deny the truth as he saw it. At the same time, however, he found support in an unexpected quarter: a Southern Whig. Alexander H. Stephens, coolly and rationally denounced the war, which was as popular in his home state of Georgia as it was in Illinois. In one of his rare, impulsive, and touching notes, Lincoln described to Herndon his own response to Stephens and his speech:

> I just take up my pen to say, that Mr. Stephens of Georgia, a little slim, pale-faced, consumptive man, with a voice like Logan's, has just concluded the very best speech, of an hour's length, I ever heard.
> My old, withered, dry eyes, are full of tears yet.
> If he writes it out any thing like he delivered it, our people shall see a good many copies of it. (I, 448)

With the exception of Lincoln's letters to his wife—and not always in them—this is one of the few letters that gives insight into Lincoln's occasional moments of spontaneous personal expression during the years following his recovery from melancholy. Direct, simple, unrestrained, and honest, this note, more than any other of the period, foreshadows his later acceptance of personal involvement and intuitively empathetic understanding. Phrased simply and personally in intuitively appropriate language and syntax, apparently incongruous and yet eminently appropriate, the letter is, on a lower but no less intimate note, like the great letters and speeches of the war years.

It is obvious that at the time Lincoln was permitting himself, gradually and cautiously, to become emotionally involved in his personal relationships at the same time that he continued his rational and objective grasp on public and legal affairs. He continued to keep the two carefully separated, permitting almost no public insight into the emotional aspect of his nature and only rarely revealing it to his friend Herndon. Consequently, he carried on his coolly logical, concerted attacks against the administration, the war, and the expected Democratic candidacy of Lewis Cass for the Presidency that year, while he wrote touchingly, with a reluctant, shy tenderness, to Mary, who had returned to Kentucky, that he missed and was concerned for her: "And you are entirely free from head-ache? That is good—good—considering it is the first spring you have been free from it since we were acquainted. I am afraid you will get so well, and fat, and young, as to be wanting to marry again. Tell Louisa I want her to watch you a little for me. Get weighed, and write me how much you weigh" (I, 466).

In the midst of such tender concern, typical of his attitude toward his wife even under trying emotional circumstances, his old fears of closeness and of the dangers inherent in intimate and affectionate human relations remained to torture him, even in dreams: "I did not get rid of the impression of that foolish dream about dear Bobby till I got your letter written the same day. What did he and Eddy think of the little letters father sent them? Don't let the blessed fellows forget father" (I, 466). Such moments of paternal concern and fear are buried in the routine of domestic trivia in the letter, as though Lincoln were reluctant to express them; and in none of the letters to Mary is there any evidence of passion. But his concern for Mary and the boys, fears for their safety, and fears that the mutuality of affection may not last are particularly evident. Perhaps during these months of separation and of loneliness Lincoln was beginning to realize that he could not live without human intimacy and that such a relationship could not be maintained on a rational basis. The cool, ambitious young man who had deliberately cut his family ties in order to follow his ambitions, who feared and fled from personal emotional involvement with others, who still did not hesitate to use his full intellectual and satirical armament upon a political opponent with every intention of destroying him, had become a solicitous and concerned husband and father.

*". . . he was elected to the lower house of Congress,
and served one term only . . ."*

The inevitable result of this separation and apprehension was, therefore, a new dimension in his thinking and writing. But still that added dimension remained isolated from his public career. An ultimate fusion of public and private concern and of the intellectual and emotional dimensions was still either unnecessary or impossible for Lincoln to achieve. But gradually his absence from his family and a growing fatherly concern for William Herndon, to whom he gave much unsolicited advice, began to draw him out. He was, as the letters make clear, gaining a maturity of insight and control that he had not known before. But he called it "getting old."

In Congress he continued his opposition to the war; he supported the Whig position on internal improvements and the tariff; he maintained his opposition to slavery; and in the summer of 1848 he spoke widely in the vicinity of Washington and in New England in support of General Taylor, the Whig Presidential candidate, who was, ironically, a hero in a war opposed by the Whigs. But Lincoln's political convictions were intellectual positions, and he treated them as such, employing the rhetorical tools that he had learned to use on the political stump and in the courtrooms of Illinois. Wit, ridicule, cross-examination, rational analysis, logical argument, and withering satire were used effectively and interchangeably as he sought to make his words as functional and forceful as possible.

V   *The Attack on Cass*

During these years in Congress Lincoln reached his peak as a stump speaker; in future campaigns he was more frequently to be a detached statesman. But in 1848 he was an obscure Western congressman in his first—and, he knew, only—term in Congress; and he was determined to make a major political impact in the way he knew best. On July 27 he rose in the House to give, in an allotted hour, what was to be his major political speech of that Presidential campaign year. He was at his best as he used the full range of his political talents in attacking the Democrats, particularly their apparent candidate General Cass, and in supporting the candidacy of General Taylor, largely unknown politically. Taylor was a Whig and a hero as William Henry Harrison had been in 1840. The Whigs had made of Harrison what they would, and they had won; and they were determined to do the same in 1848 with the hero of the war that they insisted was unconstitutional. But Cass was also a military hero, and Lincoln was determined to destroy his chance for the Presidency by making his reputation politically ineffective. In many ways Lincoln anticipated his attack against Douglas a decade later as he rose, rational, satirical, and eloquent, to the attack.

One of the most widely ranging and yet carefully controlled political speeches that Lincoln ever gave, that of July 27 was firmly rooted in the frontier stump tradition; but it went far beyond its origin in the effectiveness with which Lincoln, deliberately the skeptical Westerner, employed the techniques he had been perfecting for so long. The result—heard, read, and approved by influential Whigs from all over the country—was ultimately to have an influence Lincoln could not have anticipated; but it is obvious that he regarded it as a major political effort.

The speech, later printed in the *Congressional Globe Appendix* and subsequently reprinted as a campaign pamphlet, is divided into two major parts. The first points out, as much for the benefit of dubious Whigs as for skeptical Democrats, the suitability of Taylor as a Whig candidate for the Presidency; and the second is a strong satirical attack on the candidacy of Cass. In the first section Lincoln made Taylor's position the Whig one on the role of the Presidential veto, the tariff, currency, and internal movements. The Whig positions on these issues, he insisted, were the only logical American policies, each of which agreed with the political philosophy of the founding fathers. The Presidential veto, used freely by the Democrats and denounced by the Whigs, would, he insisted, be used by Taylor with the careful reluctance advocated by Jefferson rather than with the undemocratic abandon of Jackson and Van Buren.

In this section of the speech Lincoln applied his rapid cross-examination technique, supplemented by logical analysis and supported by impressive and weighty documentary evidence. The purpose and the effect of the approach were to force the Democrats off balance and keep them there. Finally, he reduced the argument to simple, fundamental, penetrating questions, as he was to do in debating Douglas; but in this instance he supplied his own answers, or, more properly, the answers that Taylor presumably would give. Taylor's position was simple,

". . . he was elected to the lower house of Congress,
and served one term only . . ."

Lincoln asserted; he would follow the will of the people as it
was made known by their elected representatives. There would
be no reckless, indiscriminate, undemocratic use of the veto:

> Now this is the whole matter. In substance, it is this: The
> people say to Gen: Taylor "If you are elected, shall we have a
> national bank?" He answers "*Your* will, gentlemen, not *mine*"
> "What about the Tariff?" "Say yourselves." "Shall our rivers and
> harbours be improved?" "Just as you please" "If you desire a
> bank, an alteration of the tariff, internal improvements, any, or
> all, I will not hinder you; if you do not desire them, I will not
> attempt to force them on you.". . . Now can there be any diffi-
> culty in understanding this? To you democrats, it may not seem
> like principle; but surely you cannot fail to perceive the position
> plainly enough. (I, 503-4)

Taylor, according to Lincoln, would embody the people's will,
serving only to execute it. But, it becomes evident, Taylor's position was secondary. This exposition of the position of a still
largely unknown and uncommitted candidate was prefatory to
Lincoln's major purpose: a bitingly satirical and genuinely funny
attack, in the frontier tradition, upon Cass himself. Never able
or willing to remain on the defensive in political debate, Lincoln
used Democratic accusations that the Whigs were using Taylor's
military coattails to hide under as the point of departure for his
attack. Not only had the Democrats used Jackson's coattails for
years, he pointed out, but they planned to do the same thing,
"Like a horde of hungry ticks," in 1848. He then turned to attack
the expanding coattails of General Cass:

> But in my hurry I was very near closing on the subject of mili-
> tary tails before I was done with it. There is one entire article of
> the sort I have not discussed yet; I mean the military tail you
> democrats are now engaged in dovetailing onto the great Michi-
> gander. Yes sir, all his biographers (and they are legion) have
> him in hand, tying him to a military tail, like so many mischie-
> vous boys tying a dog to a bladder of beans. True, the material
> they have is very limited; but they drive at it, might and main.
> He *in*vaded Canada without resistance, and he *out*vaded it with-
> out pursuit. As he did both under orders, I suppose there was,
> to him, neither credit nor discredit in them; but they [are made
> to] constitute a large part of the tail. He was volunteer aid to
> Gen: Harrison on the day of the battle of the Thames; and, as

you said in 1840, Harrison was picking huckleberries [whortle-
berries] two miles off while the battle was fought, I suppose it is
a just conclusion with you, to say Cass was aiding Harrison to
pick huckleberries [picking whortleberries]. This is about all,
excepted the mooted question of the broken sword. Some authors
say he broke it, some say he threw it away, and some others, who
ought to know, say nothing about it. Perhaps it would be a fair
historical compromise to say, if he did not break it, he didn't do
any thing else with it.[3]

This pointed but light satire, effectively and colloquially designed to attack the Democrats' projection of their candidate as
that of the common man, dedicated to principle and distinguished in the popular Western and Southern War of 1812,
neatly turns the tables on the opposition. Lincoln uses the arguments advanced by the Democrats to detract from the reputation
of Harrison, the Whig pseudo-frontiersman, in 1840, to destroy that of Cass, the genuine but aging Democratic frontiersman of 1848. Most effective, however, was Lincoln's ability to
make the opposition ridiculous, and he was not yet finished.
Turning then to his own humble career in the Black Hawk War,
he carried Cass down with him by laughing at himself and Cass
at the same time. In portraying himself as a bumbler, he makes
Cass the same:

By the way, Mr. Speaker, did you know I am a military hero?
Yes sir; in the days of the Black Hawk war, I fought, bled, and
came away. Speaking of Gen: Cass' career reminds me of my
own. I was not at Stillman's defeat, but I was about as near it, as
Cass was to Hulls surrender; and, like him, I saw the place very
soon afterwards. It is quite certain I did not break my sword, for
I had none to break; but I bent a musket pretty badly on one
occasion. If Cass broke his sword, the idea is, he broke it in
de[s]peration; I bent the musket by accident. If Gen: Cass went
in advance of me in picking huckleberries [whortleberries], I
guess I surpassed him in charges upon the wild onions. If he saw
any live, fighting Indians, it was more than I did; but I had a
good many bloody struggles with the musquetoes; and, although
I never fainted from loss of blood, I can truly say I was often
very hungry. Mr. Speaker, if I should ever conclude to doff whatever I suppose there is of black cockade federalism about me,
and thereupon, they shall take me up as their candidate for the

Presidency, I protest they shall not make fun of me, as they have
of Gen: Cass, by attempting to write me into a military hero.
(I, 509–10)

The delightfully colloquial flavor of this portion of the speech
—so seemingly artless and naïve—is one of the most skillful pieces
of writing in all of Lincoln's works. Not only had Lincoln made
Cass the focal point of his wit by seeming to aim at himself, but
he had effectively made ridiculous the Democratic assertions
that the Whigs were the party of reactionary, wealthy Eastern
federalism, while the Democrats were the champions of the people by presenting himself as both a genuine Whig and a genuine
bumbling frontier Brother Jonathan. This tactic was not new
with the Whigs; it had been developed in the campaign that
attempted to make Davy Crockett a genuine frontier Whig
through a long series of political tales and books ostensibly by
him, and it had been used successfully in electing Harrison,
together with his log cabin and hard cider, in 1840. But those
political images were political frauds; and Lincoln knew that
his impeccable Western background, mannerisms, speech, humor,
wit, incisiveness, and seeming naïveté were genuine. In this
speech perhaps Lincoln knew that he was presenting himself on
the national scene as the kind of candidate the Whigs must seek
in the future, but he could not know that he was laying the
foundation for the campaign of Honest Abe, the rail splitter from
Illinois, in the campaign of 1860. He was, however, clearly indi-
cating the path his political career would take in the future. The
irony of Lincoln, the primitive humorist from the prairies, with
a black federalist cockade in his hat was too good to omit, as
was the spectacle of himself as the ideal candidate for the Democrats as they saw themselves. But there is no irony in the fact
that here it appears that Lincoln rather than Taylor is the candidate opposing Cass.

Most of the remainder of the speech was an anticlimax. Lincoln castigated Cass's hesitancy and indecision on the Wilmot
Proviso, politically dangerous to the Democrats; and he attacked
Cass's public record, portraying him as a man magnificent in his
greedy appetite. Then, after attempting to rationalize and make
consistent the Whig position on the war as it related to Taylor's
heroism and candidacy, he concluded, in the character of the
frontier realist this time, with a final attack:

Mr. Speaker, I see I have but three minutes left, and this forces me to throw out one whole branch of my subject. A single word on still another. The democrats are kind enough to frequently remind us that we have some dissensions in our ranks. Our good friend from Baltimore, immediately before me (Mr. McLane) expressed some doubt the other day as to which branch of our party, Gen: Taylor would ultimately fall into the hands of. That was a new idea to me. I knew [that] we had dissenters, but I did not know they were trying to get our candidate away from us. I would like to say a word to our dissenters, but I have not the time. Some such *we* certainly have; have *you* none, gentlemen democrats? Is it all union and harmony in *your* ranks?—no bickerings?—no divisions? If there be doubt as to which of our divisions will get our candidate, is there no doubt as to which of your candidates will get your party? I have heard some things from New-York; and if they are true, one might well say of your party there, as a drunken fellow once said when he heard the reading of an indictment for hog-stealing. The clerk read on till he got to, and through the words "did steal, take, and carry away, ten boars, ten sows, ten shoats, and ten pigs" at which he exclaimed "Well, by golly, that is the most evenly divided gang of hogs, I ever did hear of." If there is any *other* gang of hogs more equally divided than the democrats of New-York are about this time, I have not heard of it. (I, 516)

As an exercise in political composition, this speech was superb. Carefully balanced, it not only covered the range of campaign debate by presenting Taylor as a model of democratic propriety and Cass as a fraud; but it was also careful to prevent any possible conclusion that Lincoln, in spite of his wit, was anything but a shrewd, incisive frontier political realist. The effect was, as Lincoln intended it to be, a major campaign document, having its effects and making its author known far beyond Congress. At the same time, it marked the climax of his career as a congressman.

During September and October, 1848, Lincoln spent much of his time stumping for Taylor, first in New England and then in Illinois, giving New England a fair sample of the Lincoln style as he had perfected it in the West. The substance of his speeches was, for the most part, that of his congressional speech; but in New England he gave more attention to his favorite theory on slavery—the recognition of its constitutionality in spite of its

moral evil and the assertion that its containment was equally
constitutional. Reactions varied; to the Whigs, his speeches,
". . . for sound reasoning, cogent argument, and keen satire, we
have seldom heard equalled."[4] To the Democrats "The speaker
was far inferior as a reasoner to others who hold the same
views, but then he was more unscrupulous, more facetious and
with his sneers he mixed up a good deal of humor. His awkward
gesticulations, the ludicrous management of his voice and the
comical expression of his countenance, all conspired to make his
audience laugh at the mere anticipation of the joke before it
appeared."[5]

However, Lincoln's New England trip was a success; and, as
he returned to Illinois, he left behind him a favorable impression
among his fellow Whigs. He also left behind the diametrically
opposed estimates of his character, personality, and ability that
were to follow him throughout the rest of his life, giving strength
to his supporters and vituperative arguments to those who opposed him, as they provided inspiration for a decade of political
caricaturists.

VI *The Niagara Fragment*

He returned to Illinois by train and Great Lakes steamer,
arriving in Buffalo on September 28 and departing on the *Globe*
on September 1. An obscure congressman stopping at Niagara
Falls, like thousands of other mid-nineteenth-century tourists,
elicited no comment; it was simply the thing to do. However,
Lincoln's visit to the Falls resulted in a controversy among those
biographers and historians who have sought to interpret him.
But the controversy itself is unimportant; the actual significance
of his visit and subsequent steamer trip home is that they combine to emphasize the dichotomy that is the central paradox of
the man, his thinking, and his writing, perplexing to so many
who sought to see in Lincoln only what reflected themselves.

Some time after his return, as William Herndon recounts, he
and Lincoln fell to discussing the Falls, which Herndon had also
recently visited. After attempting and failing to describe the
terrifying grandeur that the sight was to him, Herndon recalled,
he turned to Lincoln and asked, "What . . . made the deepest impression on you when you stood in the presence of the great nat-

ural wonder?" Lincoln's reply was laconically matter-of-fact:
" 'The thing that struck me most forcefully when I saw the Falls,'
he responded, 'was, where in the world did all that water come
from.' "[6]

To Herndon, this exchange provided insight into Lincoln's
personality and mind; he had, Herndon asserted, ". . . no eye for
the magnificence and grandeur of the scene . . . ,"[7] no insight into
the metaphysical wonder before him, no poetic imagination. Instead, Herndon asserted, Lincoln demonstrated here the source
of his power: a keen, rational mind that stripped away all emotional and verbal superfluities in order to penetrate to the factual
basis of the wonder.

Obviously Lincoln was teasing the matter-of-fact, humorless
Herndon, as he often did, knowing that Herndon considered
himself Lincoln's superior in culture. But a document survives,
a fragment of an essay, that reveals the dichotomy in Lincoln's
nature as it was becoming increasingly evident in the late 1840's.
The fragment reveals, too, that Lincoln was moving closer to the
ability to forge a complete statement that begins in fact and ends
in reverence and wonder. The essay began with the rational
curiosity that Herndon described, but it then revealed that for
the first time Lincoln had begun to realize that such rationality
is insignificant, even meaningless in the face of timelessness. The
fragment remained uncompleted because Lincoln had not yet
learned, in spite of, or perhaps because of, his poetic experiments, to express that reverence and emotional commitment in
the same simple profundities in which he clothed his personal
feelings. He wrote:

Niagara Falls! By what mysterious power is it that millions and
millions, are drawn from all parts of the world, to gaze upon
Niagara Falls? There is no mystery about the thing itself. Every
effect is just such as any intiligent man knowing the causes,
would anticipate, without [seeing] it. If the water moving onward in a great river, reaches a point where there is a perpen-
dicular jog, of a hundred feet in descent, in the bottom of the
river,—it is plain the water will have a violent and continuous
plunge at that point. It is also plain the water, thus plunging, will
foam, and roar, and send up a mist, continuously, in which last,
during sunshine, there will be perpetual rain-bows. The mere
physical of Niagara Falls is only this. Yet this is really a very

small part of that world's wonder. It's power to excite reflection,
and emotion, is it's charm. The geologist will demonstrate that
the plunge, or fall, was once at Lake Ontario, and has worn it's
way back to it's present position; he will ascertain how *fast* it is
wearing now, and so get a basis for determining how long it has
been wearing back from Lake Ontario, and finally demonstrate
by it that this world is at least fourteen thousand years old. A
philosopher of a slightly different turn will say Niagara Falls is
only the lip of the basin out of which pours all the surplus water
which rains down on two or three hundred thousand square miles
of the earth's surface. He will estim[ate with] approximate accu-
racy, that five thousand [to]ns of water, falls with it's full weight,
a distance of a hundred feet each minute—thus exerting a force
equal to the lifting of the same weight, through the same space,
in the same time. And then the further reflection comes that this
vast amount of water, constantly pouring *down,* is supplied by
an equal amount constantly *lifted up,* by the sun; and still he says,
"If this amount is lifted up, for *this one* space of two or three hundred thousand square miles, an equal amount must be lifted for
every other equal space"; and he is overwhelmed in the contem-
plation of the vast power the sun is constantly exerting in quiet,
noiseless operation of lifting water *up* to be rained *down* again.
   But still there is more. It calls up the indefinite past. When
Columbus first sought this continent—when Christ suffered on
the cross—when Moses led Israel through the Red-Sea—nay; even
when Adam first came from the hand of his Maker—then as now,
Niagara was roaring here. The eyes of that species of extinct
giants, whose bones fill the mounds of America, have gazed on
Niagara, as ours do now. Co[n]temporary with the whole race of
men, and older than the first man, Niagara is strong and fresh
today as ten thousand years ago. The Mammoth and Mastadon—
now so long dead, that fragments of their monstrous bones, alone
testify, that they ever lived, have gazed on Niagara. In that long
—long time, never still for a single moment. Never dried, never
froze, never slept, never rested. (II, 10–11)

Unpolished and unfinished, ending abruptly in the middle of
a sentence, Lincoln's attempt to define the meaning of Niagara
Falls is certainly insignificant as literature when compared with
the similar accounts written by literary travelers of the nineteenth century. It reveals neither the Lincoln of the Gettysburg
Address nor the unimaginative lawyer portrayed by Herndon. It
does show, however, that Lincoln did wonder where all that

water came from and that he had made it his business to try to find out, just as his observations of the stranded steamboat on that trip and his experience with a stranded boat on the Sangamon years before led, in 1849, to a patented and practical if somewhat unwieldy device for freeing stranded steamers. This man was the Lincoln who rose from poverty to a then modest and later great success through his own determination, practical insight, and sharp native intelligence.

But the description of Niagara Falls reveals the man who, in the face of that wonder, felt something beyond rational observation and analysis; who glimpsed, however fleetingly, a moment of eternity in the onrushing water; and who tried unsuccessfully to record it. In the rolling cadence of the last line there are overtones, rudimentary but no less real, of the permanence connoted with crystal clarity in the Gettysburg Address. Perhaps the fragment was unfinished because, like its far greater successor, it was finished; and Lincoln knew that there was nothing more to be said. More probably, however, Lincoln recognized the inadequacy of his verbal skill to convey what he felt to be true beyond what rationality would support. Certainly he was moving slowly but perceptibly toward recognition of that awareness in himself and toward gaining the power necessary to express it.

Lincoln returned to Washington in December for the second session; but the excitement of a Presidential election year was gone, and he knew that it was to be his last congressional experience. Jubilant over Taylor's election, confident that his loyalty and services would be rewarded, he found nevertheless that the second session was comparatively dull. But, with Presidential politics out of the way, much of his attention during those final months was directed toward the limitation of slavery by attempting to exclude it from the newly annexed territories and by eliminating it from the District of Columbia.

On December 24 he sent twenty dollars to his father, who had had John D. Johnson write that the farm was in danger of foreclosure; and he wrote a moralistic letter to Johnston, who had requested eighty dollars, pleading poverty, helplessness, and despair. In both letters Lincoln cited his willingness to be helpful; but at the same time he pointed out that wasteful carelessness rather than laziness or deliberate improvidence was the cause of both men's predicaments. His acceptance of the Protestant Ethic, undoubtedly the basis of his Whiggish economic conservatism, is nowhere more evident. His letter to his father was restrained, but to Johnston he was blunt:

> . . . Now this can only happen by some defect in your *conduct.* What that defect is, I think I know. You are not *lazy,* and still you *are* an *idler.* I doubt whether since I saw you, you have done a good whole day's work, in any one day. You do not very much dislike to work; and still you do not work much, merely because it does not seem to you that you could get much for it. This habit of uselessly wasting time is the whole difficulty. . . . (II, 16)

Combined with this analysis was a proposal that Johnston go to work and that Lincoln would match every dollar he earned before the first of May with another. This solution to Johnston's financial predicament was both practical and moral; it would, if carried out, get Johnston out of debt and at the same time encourage proper work habits. In concluding, however, Lincoln reverted to his habit of demolishing his opponent's position before ending with an appeal for the acceptance of his own:

> You say you would almost give your place in Heaven for $70 or $80. Then you value your place in Heaven very cheaply for I am sure you can with the offer I make you get the seventy or eighty dollars for four or five months work. You say if I furnish you the money you will deed me the land, and, if you don't pay the money back, you will deliver possession. Nonsense! If you cant now live *with* the land, how will you then live without it? You have always been [kind] to me, and I do not now mean to be unkind to you. On the contrary, if you will but follow my advice, you will find it worth more than eight times eighty dollars to you. (II, 16)

Lincoln's proposal was not without kindness or good intent, and the letter suggests that Lincoln knew Johnston's character well enough to impose such conditions. But more important was his confidence that Johnston also could rise if he were determined and willing to work. Lincoln, although sentimental or emotional toward his wife and sons during those years, remained convinced that other human problems—whether his father's and Johnston's or the nation's—could best be solved by logical analysis and a rational solution. At the same time that he presented such a solution to Johnston, he proposed to approach the slavery problem in the same way. Although the problem was human in origin, he saw it manifested in legal and constitutional terms, and he was convinced that it could only be resolved on that basis. To argue in terms of morality rather than reason he considered ill-advised and useless.

On January 10 and February 13, 1849, he made his last important appearances on the House floor. The first occasion was to propose an amendment to an instruction given to the House Committee on the District of Columbia to prepare a bill abolishing slavery in the District. The amendment was in effect a proposed bill providing for the abolishment of slavery in the District with the consent of the voters and with compensation for the owners. Furthermore, as Lincoln implemented it, it would grant automatic freedom to children of slave mothers born after January 1, 1850, and it would provide for return to their owners of slaves who had escaped into the District from slave states.

Lincoln's only major attempt to limit slavery while he was in Congress, it came to nothing, as did all such bills; but it elicited much favorable comment from sympathizers. The political strategy of Lincoln, a lame-duck freshman congressman introducing such a bill at that time is questionable; but, clearly phrased, avoiding ambiguities and circumlocutions, it made his opinion of the institution and his concept of a logical means whereby the problem might be attacked a matter of public record.

On February 13 he commented on the disposition of public lands to encourage development, important to him both as a frontiersman interested in such development and as a Whig protective of private enterprise. But during these last months he was preparing to leave and to attempt to construct a future; his term was to expire as Taylor took office. Looking for well-earned patronage, he sought to become Commissioner of the General Land Office, later returning to Washington to plead his case with Taylor, but he was not selected.

Busy recommending positions for others, it appeared that he would get none; and late in March he returned to Springfield to his law practice. Still convinced that Illinois should have a high patronage office and that it should be his, he continued his efforts, supported by his friends. He was reluctant to leave public life, but it appeared that he was destined to do so. However,

[98]

". . . he was elected to the lower house of Congress,
and served one term only . . ."

in September he was offered the governorship of Oregon Territory, which was soon to become a state, in which Lincoln could become a political power. The offer appeared to be an excellent opportunity, but it meant a return to the frontier; and Lincoln, supported by his wife, turned it down. He chose instead increasing prosperity and security in his Illinois law practice—an important decision.

CHAPTER *5*

". . . he went to the practice of law with greater earnestness than ever before . . ."

IN 1848 the Whigs had elected their second President in less than a decade, and the future of the party seemed secure. But Taylor, like Harrrison, was elected on the basis of his personal appeal as a hero rather than the popularity of his policies or his party. By 1850 the party was doomed; the apparent political unity that had secured Taylor's election was illusory. Taylor's death in 1850 gave the Presidency to Millard Fillmore, who, unlike John Tyler, who had served almost all of Harrison's term, kept the Whig faith; but the party itself was suffering from the same disease that afflicted the nation. In 1848 many Whigs had become Free-Soilers, and within the party "Conscience Whigs" battled "Cotton Whigs" over the slavery issue. By 1852 these disputes rendered the party almost impotent; its nominee, another general, Winfield Scott, was defeated decisively; and new political alignments began to be made.

Hastening the end of the party were the deaths of its great leaders. On February 24, 1848, Lincoln had been on the House committtee to oversee the funeral preparations for John Quincy Adams, whom he had seen stricken on the House floor; on July 25, 1850, he memorialized Zachary Taylor in Chicago; and on July 6, 1852, he delivered a eulogy in the Illinois House of Representatives on the death of Henry Clay. Deprived of its leadership and unable to resolve the intraparty dispute that was bigger than all parties, the Whig party continued to exist in name after it ceased existing in fact. Lincoln had campaigned for Scott, although without the enthusiasm of past years; and, perhaps unwilling to accept the death of his party and surely waiting to see what remained after the dust had settled, he was one of the decreasing number who continued to consider themselves

Whigs. But he concentrated his energies on building the law practice of Lincoln and Herndon, his political career apparently over.

The decade of the 1850's was the most dramatic, most fateful in American history, a period of high drama that moved inexorably toward its climax. Opened by the Compromise of 1850 that served to deepen rather than heal wounds, as Clay had anticipated, the decade included the Kansas-Nebraska Act, the Dred Scott decision, and overt and covert warfare in Kansas; and it was concluded by John Brown's raid and his martyrdom. Lincoln, who determined to remain aloof, was a political combatant of strong opinions by nature; and he, like thousands of others, was drawn onto the eventful stage. Lincoln, however, was destined to play the major role in the last act in the 1860's.

During the first years of the 1850's Lincoln's second son Eddie died after a lingering illness, and two more sons were born. As a family man and as a lawyer, determined to succeed in the role fate had placed him, he became prominent and popular on the judicial circuit of central Illinois, his fame as a shrewd lawyer and good companion traveling beyond it. But his political star had apparently set, while that of Stephen Douglas, his old rival, continued to rise on the national scene as he strove desperately to stave off the inevitable break in the Democratic party and the nation by compromising conscience with political reality and expediency. Popular sovereignty was the means by which Douglas sought to unit his party and to save the country; it would, he was convinced, solve the slavery issue and heal sectional wounds at the same time. But to Lincoln and others who opposed that solution, it meant the probability of a victory for slavery, a resurgence that would give the institution new political power through expansion; and they were convinced that the slave power had to be stopped. Positive political action was the only acceptable means by which it could be done.

By 1856 Lincoln was a Republican, a member of a loose political alliance of men with no common political philosophy except a dislike for slavery but with no common idea of what could be done to prevent its expansion or hasten its extinction. But the two years before 1856 were important. Lincoln's position on slavery had remained unchanged since his youth, and he had begun to move toward the Republicans in September and October,

1854, with a series of speeches denouncing the repeal of the Missouri Compromise in the Nebraska Act, which "... aroused him as he had never been before ..." (IV, 67). Once again he was in the political arena, not as a partisan party member, but as an indignant citizen whose major political aim was to secure the re-election of his friend Richard Yates to Congress. But that series of speeches was in effect the first round in the Lincoln-Douglas debates; Lincoln emerged from the campaign elected once more to the Illinois General Assembly. Again he had become a major political activist, a role he was not to relinquish.

I *The Anti-Nebraska Fight*

In the anti-Nebraska speeches of 1854 Lincoln clashed directly with Douglas at the State Fair on October 4 and in Peoria on October 16; then they agreed to meet directly no more in that campaign. The text of the first speech has been lost, but the summary in the *Illinois Journal* the next day indicates that Lincoln had lost none of his skill, for he had advanced arguments against popular sovereignty developed through homely analogies as he had in the past and was to do again. Logic, tradition, the Constitution, and common sense were opposed to repealing the Missouri Compromise, he declared: "If I have a field ... around which the cattle or hogs linger and crave to pass the fence, and I go and tear down the fence, will it be supposed that I do not by that act encourage them to enter? *Even the hogs would know better*—Much more *men*, who are a higher order of the animal world."[1]

At Peoria, Douglas had spent three hours explaining and defending the Nebraska Act, and Lincoln was determined to spend as much time opposing it. The result, a refutation and denial reviewing the entire controversy, was one of Lincoln's longest political speeches; but it was carefully organized, developed, and supported. Determined to make his own position clear at the beginning, he reiterated his analysis of the difference between slavery as it existed and as it attempted expansion. In his opening remarks was an acknowledgment that he proposed a national rather than regional or local solution. Douglas' bill was, in effect, an attempt to minimize the issue by denationalizing it, making it a state or territorial matter; Lincoln, however, recog-

nized that the only possible solution must be national, in terms
of nationally accepted definitions of union, liberty, and democracy, rather than state or regional definitions. "I ... wish to be
no less than National in all the positions I may take; and when-
ever I take ground which others have thought, or may think,
narrow, sectional, and dangerous to the Union, I hope to give a
reason, which will appear sufficient, at least to some, why I think
differently" (II, 248).

Aware that the course he pursued was potentially dangerous
to the Union and to himself, unlike Douglas' appeal to traditional state and local democratic sentiments, Lincoln proceeded
to outline a reasoned position from which he never deviated in
principle. In the process, as he had done so often before, he cut
through to the crucial question at the heart of the problem:

> The doctrine of self government is right—absolutely and eter-
> nally right—but it has no just application, as here attempted. Or
> perhaps I should rather say that whether it has such just appli-
> cation depends upon whether a negro is *not* or *is* a man. If he is
> *not* a man, why in that case, he who *is* a man may, as a matter
> of self-government, do just as he pleases with him. But if the
> negro *is* a man, is it not to that extent, a total destruction of self-
> government, to say that he too shall not govern *himself?* When
> the white man governs himself that is self-government; but when
> he governs himself, and also governs *another* man, that is *more*
> than self-government—that is despotism. If the negro is a *man,*
> why then my ancient faith teaches me that "all men are created
> equal;" and there can be no moral right in connection with one
> man's making a slave of another. (II, 265–66)

Like Douglas, Lincoln sought a solution to the problem in
terms of the democratic ideal, but their concepts of that ideal
were opposed. Douglas sought the simplistic solution inherent in
the Jacksonian principle of majority rule; but Lincoln, in many
respects the heir of the Federalist tradition of John Adams, was
acutely aware of the ever-present possibility of tyranny of the
majority, especially evident in the slaveholding areas. Both men,
consequently, were democratic and anti-democratic at the same
time: Douglas, because he would permit the democratic majority
to assert property rights in human beings if they chose to do so;
Lincoln, because he would deny them that right. But to Lincoln
human rights were superior to property rights, even if a majority

supported property rights. An intellectual position derived from the American eighteenth-century ideal, it was, Lincoln believed, destined to become the American reality in the nineteenth century.

Lincoln continued his opposition to Douglas' bill with attacks throughout the fall and early winter of 1854, and in the campaign he realized that he was back in politics to stay, with a cause that transcended any he had supported before. On December 1 he confessed that discovery to his friend Joseph Gillespie:

> I have really got it into my head to try to be United States Senator; and if I could have your support my chances would be reasonably good. But I know, and acknowledge, that you have as just claims to the place as I have; and therefore I do not ask you to yield to me, if you are thinking of becoming a candidate yourself. If, however, you are not, then I should like to be remembered affectionately by you; and also, to have you make a mark for me with the Anti-Nebraska members down your way.
> (II, 290)

Lincoln's chances did indeed seem good; although the Whig party was in disorder, the strong Democratic party was hardly better off, with a number of them now known as anti-Nebraska Democrats. Lincoln resigned from the legislature in order to seek the support of both Whigs and anti-Nebraska men. To the latter he stressed the fact that they were on the same side on that crucial issue. But the anti-Nebraska Democrats stood firm, and after the campaign he had to write:

> The election is over, the Session is ended, and I am *not* Senator. I have to content myself with the honor of having been the first choice of a large majority of the fiftyone members who finally made the election. My larger number of friends had to surrender to Trumbull's smaller number, in order to prevent the election of Matteson, which would have been a Douglas victory. I started with 44 votes & T. with 5. It was rather hard for the 44 to have to surrender to the 5—and a less good humored man than I, perhaps, would not have consented to it—and it would not have been done without my consent. I could not, however, let the whole political result go to ruin, on a point merely personal to myself.
> (II, 360–7)

Although he had not been elected to the United States Senate, Lincoln consoled himself with the knowledge that Douglas's man had also lost; and another anti-Nebraska voice would go to the Senate. From this point the campaign lines in Illinois were drawn as they were to remain for the rest of the decade and as they spread to include the nation by 1860. Douglas, nationally known, respected, and seen as a certain Democratic heir to the Presidency, and Lincoln, little known outside his home state, were to debate for the next six years; and in the process Lincoln was to prevent Douglas' election to the Presidency while insuring his own. But, to do so, he had to re-examine his political principles; abandon his Whig party; and join forces with the men who were banding together to fight for the preservation of the Missouri Compromise. By May, 1856, he had declared himself a member of the new Republican party, determined to oppose what he saw as certain expansion of slavery.

Important in leading him to make this decision were two factors. The first was a resurgence, with an intensity that he had not known since he was a boy, of a belief in the righteousness and justice of God. The other was a sudden, deep insight into the magnitude of the problem facing the country. This realization led him to understand the ultimate question behind the crisis, a question the implications of which disturbed but did not deter him.

II *The Resurgence of Religious Belief*

The return to religious faith was marked neither by sectarianism nor emotionalism, but it was deeply fundamental in its profound confidence in the role of God in human affairs. Perhaps initiated by the death of his son Eddie on February 1, 1850, that faith was most evident in Lincoln's letter to John D. Johnston as Thomas Lincoln, with whom Lincoln had never become reconciled, lay dying in January, 1851:

> You already know I desire that neither Father nor Mother shall be in want of any comfort either in health or sickness while they live; and I feel sure you have not failed to use my name, if necessary, to procure a doctor, or any thing else for Father in his present sickness. My business is such that I could hardly leave home now, if it were not, as it is, that my own wife is sick-abed. . . . I sincerely hope Father may yet recover his health; but at all events tell him to remember to call upon, and confide

in, our great, and good, and merciful Maker; who will not turn
away from him in any extremity. He notes the fall of a sparrow,
and numbers the hairs of our heads; and He will not forget the
dying man, who puts his trust in Him. Say to him that if we
could meet now, it is doubtful whether it would not be more
painful than pleasant; but that if it be his lot to go now, he will
soon have a joyous [meeting] with many loved ones gone before;
and where [the rest] of us, through the help of God, hope ere-
long [to join] them.[2]

Lincoln's faith, combined with his fatalism, remained on this
level to the end, fusing confidence, wonder, and resignation, as it
manifested itself in growing concern for the future of the nation
and as, in his last months, he pondered the meaning of the war
and tried to define it for the nation and himself. But his recognition of the role of God in the affairs of the nation began to
become evident in 1855 as he re-examined his long-held position
on slavery in the light of the intensified struggle over freedom
in Kansas.

III *The Heart of the Crisis*

He had long believed that slavery was wrong but that it was
sanctioned by the Constitution; consequently, he felt, it could
not be interfered with where it already existed. But he was convinced that constitutionally it could be prevented from expanding and that morally it must be. Much of his opposition to the
Mexican War was based on this premise as was his fight against
popular sovereignty for states and territories declared free by
the Missouri Compromise of 1820. But he saw both slavery and
anti-slavery on the offensive, with slavery in the ascendancy; and
in the summer of 1855 he came to a frightening conclusion and
a humble admission that led to a new position that he maintained to the end. In a letter to Judge George Robertson of Lex-
ington, Kentucky, he outlined the political problem facing the
nation, a problem that had grown out of the slave crisis, but that
outweighed slavery in its implications for the future:

> You are not a friend of slavery in the abstract. In that speech
> you spoke of *"the peaceful extinction of slavery"* and used other
> expressions indicating your belief that the thing was, at some
> time, to have an end[.] Since then we have had thirty six years

of experience; and this experience has demonstrated, I think, that
there is no peaceful extinction of slavery in prospect for us. . . .
The Fourth of July has not quite dwindled away; it is still a
great day—*for burning fire-crackers*!!! . . .
   Our political problem now is "Can we, as a nation, continue
together *permanently—forever*—half slave and half free?" The
problem is too mighty for me. May God, in his mercy, super-
intend the solution. (II, 318)

This statement is the basis of the "House Divided" attack that
Lincoln was to launch and sustain during the campaign of 1858.
But in 1855 it was neither a surrender to an imponderable, impossible problem nor a policy. Instead, it was the point of departure for a new concept that he was to carry on into the
political wars of the rest of the decade and into the military
battles of the next.

IV   *The Lost Speech*

That new program was outlined in the so-called Lost Speech
delivered at the state convention of the Republican party at
Bloomington, Illinois, on May 29, 1856. In it Lincoln attempted
to imbue the party with his new, all-embracing idea. Inspired
by the speeches of Daniel Webster debating Hayne and accepting the Compromise of 1850, but recognizing that Webster's
anticipation had now become fact, he spoke not only against
slavery but for the Union. The text of that speech is lost, but
the substance and its effect remain yet. Only one contemporary
account exists; matter of factly it sets the stage and summarizes
Lincoln's remarks:

Abraham Lincoln, of Sangamon, came upon the platform amid
deafening applause. He enumerated the pressing reasons of the
present movement. He was here ready to fuse with anyone who
would unite with him to oppose slave power; spoke of the bugbear
disunion which was so vaguely threatened. It was to be remembered that the *Union must be preserved in the purity of its principles as well as in the integrity of its territorial parts.* It must be
"Liberty and Union, now and forever, one and inseparable." The
sentiment in favor of white slavery now prevailed in all the slave
state papers, except those of Kentucky, Tennessee and Missouri
and Maryland. Such was the progress of the National Democracy. Douglas once claimed against him that Democracy favored

more than his principles, the individual rights of man. Was it not strange that he must stand there now to defend those rights against their former eulogist? The Black Democracy were endeavoring to cite Henry Clay to reconcile Old Whigs to their doctrine, and repaid them with the very cheap compliment of National Whigs.[3]

This prosaic account is all that remains of what was, from all contemporary comments, one of Lincoln's greatest speeches. Herndon later stated that, although he usually took down Lincoln's speeches, he "... threw away pen and paper and lived only in the inspiration of the hour";[4] and the statement aroused editorial support, including that of the Chicago *Democratic Press*. Reconstructions of the speech have been attempted, most notably that by Henry C. Whitney in 1896; but none has captured what must have been a stirring moment for the delegates as they heard Lincoln redirect their thinking from consideration of slavery as the paramount issue of the day to determination to preserve the Union. The Union was synonymous with liberty, he asserted, as the founding fathers had determined it should be eighty years before; and it had to be saved. In his speech Lincoln made a major contribution to the philosophy of the Republican party in Illinois. This was the feat that he was to attempt to duplicate for the national party at the Cooper Union four years later.

The 1856 speech had an important effect on Lincoln's personal political fortunes in his new party. At the Republican National Convention, held in Philadelphia three weeks later, his name was entered for nomination for the Vice Presidency, the second name prosposed. In the balloting he received 110 votes, a substantial number for an obscure prairie politician. The speech did not insure his nomination for the Presidency four years later, as some biographers maintain; but it did contribute to his reputation as a party leader. Although his comments on his proposed nomination were self-effacing, he made more than fifty speeches in the ensuing months for the Republican ticket of John C. Fremont and William A. Dayton.

Opposing Fremont were two candidates, Millard Fillmore, now a Know-Nothing, and James Buchanan, the Democrat. With the Democrats united behind Buchanan and the anti-Democratic forces split, Buchanan became a minority President. But Lincoln,

"... he went to the practice of law with greater earnestness
than ever before ..."

not at all disheartened, continued his political activity to the neglect of his law practice and his family. Almost at once he began the campaign to unite the anti-slavery and pro-Union forces in the Republican party, and he must have begun making plans at the same time to insure the split of the Democracy in 1860. On December 10, 1856, he pointed out what he saw as the ultimate undebatable issue: "The human heart *is* with us— God is with us. We shall again be able not to declare, that 'all States as States, are equal.' nor yet that 'all citizens as citizens are equal,' but to renew the broader, better declaration, including both these and much more, that all *men* are created equal' " (II, 385).

By this time Lincoln's concept of the growing crisis was fixed, and he was determined that the cause of liberty and union must not be compromised. The Dred Scott decision, handed down by the United States Supreme Court early in 1857, did not materially alter either his concept of the relationship between slavery and the Constitution or his conviction that the house divided against itself by slavery could not endure. It did, however, intensify his belief that the slaveholder's power was on the offensive and that it could be halted only by the election of a Republican in 1860. To that end he determined to fight Buchanan and Douglas at every opportunity. After these two split over Kansas, in effect splitting their party, Lincoln knew that Douglas would be the leading Democratic contender in 1860; and he determined to keep him from the Presidency.

Lincoln's re-entry into politics in the mid-1850's was inspired not by personal ambition, as his initial entry had been twenty years before, nor was it because he loved partisan warfare, as had been the case in the 1840's. This time it was brought about because he had found a cause growing out of a threat, and the resulting emotional commitment, stronger than anything he had ever known before, realigned his political allegiances, his thinking, and his life itself. Particularly, during these years, this commitment had a major effect on his writing: for the first time it not only maintained its basis in personal opinion, logical conviction, or *pro forma* statement, but it became increasingly imbued with moral fervor, giving it a depth it had not had before.

In the past his writing, like his thinking, had been dominated by the techniques of Western politics and the law, modified and controlled by his acceptance of the eighteenth-century rule of reason and by his use of the weapon of satire. He had been, in effect, a backwoods son of the Enlightenment, a Benjamin Franklin of the Illinois prairies; and, like Franklin, he had accepted the values of middle-class society and pursued them at the same time that he propagated them. Consequently, in spite of his often-cited liking for a bawdy joke, he was in many ways a puritan, a product of the Protestant Ethic. Hard work, thrift, and sobriety were, he believed, the mark of the virtuous man; practiced, they would result in ample reward and advancement.

Combined with his faith and certainly a product of it were his political principles—conservatism in economic affairs and liberality in society. Combined, the two would, as he saw it, provide a political and social climate in which ability would be the ultimate test of the individual's place in society. Consequently, he continually sought a national environment in which opportunity would be open to all who were willing to seek it out.

This position was a matter of faith, but it was reinforced and explained by his intellectual convictions. For all practical purposes the intellectual predominated, minimizing his sympathy for others; and on occasion, particularly in his relationship with his father and stepbrother, it led to intolerance. He had risen through his own efforts; he was determined to continue to do so; and, he was convinced, others could do the same if they had the will and the ability. The competition of life, most evident in politics, became a pleasure to him as well as the most available means by which a poor but virtuous boy might rise to the top in an open society. In seeking to rise, Lincoln had instinctively rejected the Jacksonian egalitarianism of the frontier for the natural aristocracy of a stable, orderly society; and he was determined to prove his worthiness to be part of that aristocracy.

Such a position is not conducive to sympathy with the unfortunate or tolerance for human weakness; and Lincoln, for the first forty years of his life, had little of either. His weapons in debate or in writing were logic and ridicule, and he employed them freely and skillfully. Humility, evident in his early years, became minimal; and he became dissatisfied with merely besting an opponent; he was determined to destroy him. Shrewd, ambitious, intelligent, and determined, his loyalties and his abilities were given freely to extensions of himself; and, throughout his

"... he went to the practice of law with greater earnestness than ever before ..."

active political life prior to 1850, he was a dedicated member of the political party whose ideals and his own were often interchangeable. They were positions based in logic rather than in the emotionalism of Jacksonian democracy; they were intellectual abstractions rather than flesh-and-blood realities; and he could and did accept them on that basis.

But in the early 1850's a major shift occurred. Manifesting itself at first in a determination to succeed modestly in Illinois law rather than flamboyantly in politics, it was, perhaps, the product of the rejection he felt after leaving Congress and of the personal tragedy in the death of his son—defeats that he had no power to forestall or prevent. From this point, it becomes evident, Lincoln began to find, for the first time, an emotional commitment to something greater than himself, his ambitions, and his political party. He had, in fact, found a faith that had been lost for more than a quarter century, but that he had absorbed long before he rejected the frontier, his family, and the dream that both sought in their restless movement westward.

Lincoln returned, in philosophy and conviction, to an emotional commitment to the will of God and to the equality of man —a combined faith that was proclaimed from countless frontier pulpits and stumps in his youth; and the second part, he saw clearly, was an extension of the first, a self-evident truth too long ignored or denied as an impossible good or a necessary evil. Practically and emotionally this change led to an increasing preoccupation with the prospects for the future of the nation; and he saw for it either the triumph of slavery, with freedom extinguished, or disunion. And gradually, with that growing emotional commitment, he became convinced that the Union itself— a mystic unity transcending all physical, political, and personal barriers—was the source of liberty and equality, synonymous with both. Lincoln's ambitions remained, as did his conviction that reason should prevail; but for the first time he found a cause, and he became convinced that it alone was worth serving.

If Lincoln had died at this point, he would have been forgotten and his writings would have remained political footnotes to the era in which the American nation moved toward maturity. The great statements of his Presidency were still almost a decade in the future, and he had not yet undergone the supreme trial of war that was to give them their basis in human emotion. But by

1856 the path toward them was marked out as he unleashed his long-controlled emotional intensity in the cause that led to the war and beyond.

CHAPTER 6

"Let us have faith..."

IN 1857 Lincoln was the most widely known Republican in Illinois; his reputation had spread into Indiana, Michigan, Ohio, and Missouri, as well as his native Kentucky; and he had begun to be noted by the Eastern leaders of the party. By 1858 he became the party's logical choice to oppose Douglas for the United States Senate in Illinois. Douglas' Nebraska Bill had made him unpopular with a large segment of the Democratic party in Illinois, so that Lincoln's chances for election seemed excellent. The onus of Whiggery had been removed from Lincoln through his membership in the new Republican party, to which many anti-Nebraska Democrats had given their allegiance; and he continued to work to weld the ensuing loose conglomeration into a viable political organization. Through his constant letter writing, meetings, and continual assaults on Douglas, the Nebraska Bill, and the Dred Scott decision, he sought to convince the Illinois electorate that the aggressive, expansionist policy of the slave power was an immediate threat.

This maneuver was a logical political one. Douglas was apparently the only man, of North or South, behind whom the Democrats could unite in 1860. But Lincoln was convinced that Democratic union could take place only by permitting the advance of slavery, sanctioned by the Nebraska Act, into the free states and the territories. Douglas, Lincoln knew, had sacrificed some of his Northern popularity by his stand on Nebraska and had alienated more by his apparent acceptance of the Dred Scott decision as the law of the land. Lincoln determined to exploit that breach by hammering at the issues that would widen it in Illinois, thus insuring his own election to the Senate; and he hoped later to open a breach between Douglas and the South. The result he sought was the fragmentation of the Democrats, as the Whigs had been shattered earlier; and the election of a

Republican President in 1860. Immediate strategy for the senatorial election occupied most of his attention in 1857 and 1858; but, in the course of the debates with Douglas in the fall of 1858, the election of 1860 became an increasingly important consideration.

However, Douglas' political acumen and personal integrity were equal to Lincoln's; and, when Buchanan indicated his support of the Lecompton constitution for Kansas, adopted by the pro-slavery element in that territory, Douglas, who had supported Buchanan in 1856 as a compromise candidate, denounced the Buchanan administration and the Lecompton Constitution. Both, he asserted, violated all the principles of democracy, of popular sovereignty as he believed in it. Such a stand took a great deal of personal courage, and it was a spectacular political action. The immediate result was a surge of popular sympathy for Douglas among previously alienated factions of the Northern Democracy and among Republicans.

More important, to Lincoln's dismay, was speculation among Republican leaders in the East about the possibilities of supporting Douglas in the coming elections, literally drafting him as a Republican. But it became evident that Douglas had offended the Southern Democracy, and the hoped-for split between North and South began to become evident. Lincoln determined to exploit that breach and at the same time make impossible any support of Douglas by Republicans.

I The "House Divided" Speech

The opening shot in what was to be an aggressive tactical and strategic campaign was fired by Lincoln at the Republican State Convention at Springfield in June. The outlook for Republican success was not favorable in spite of Lincoln's strong support among the old Whigs and Free-Soilers in the party. When Herndon returned from an eastern trip to sound out sentiment among the party leaders, he reported that Seward, Sumner, Philips, Garrison, and others, including Horace Greely, remained sympathetic to Douglas. Lincoln determined to destroy that sentiment by making clear what he feared would be the inevitable result of Douglas' programs. The result was his "House Divided" speech, designed to resurrect Republican fears of slave expansion by raising the emotional specter of a slaveholding nation, by analyzing the course of events that made that specter a real possibility, and then by linking Douglas irretrievably to both the events and the possibility.

Immediately he raised the issue, defining without answering the question that had haunted him as unanswerable except in terms of horror since popular sovereignty was proposed as a means of denationalizing and democratizing slavery:

> If we could first know *whether* we are, and *whither* we are tending, we could then better judge *what* to do, and *how* to do it.
>
> We are now far into the *fifth* year, since a policy was initiated, with the *avowed* object, and *confident* promise of putting an end to slavery agitation.
>
> Under the operation of that policy, that agitation has not only, not *ceased*, but has *constantly augmented*.
>
> In *my* opinion, it *will* not cease, until a crisis shall have been reached and passed.
>
> "A house divided against itself cannot stand."
>
> I believe this government cannot endure, permanently half *slave* and half *free*.
>
> I do not expect the Union to be *dissolved*—I do not expect the house to *fall*—but I *do* expect it will cease to be divided.
>
> It will become *all* one thing, or *all* the other.
>
> Either the *opponents* of slavery, will arrest the further spread of it, and place it where the public mind shall rest in the belief that it is in the course of ultimate extinction; or its *advocates* will push it forward, till it shall become alike lawful in *all* the States, *old* as well as *new*—*North* as well as *South*. (II, 461–62)

The issue and the threat were to Lincoln clear-cut: slavery could not be denationalized; it had either to grow or die. If it grew, it would devour free institutions; and the course of events since the early 1850's had encouraged that growth. Equally simple was the solution, if men were willing to seek it: if its growth were stopped through reiteration and implementation of the principles of freedom, it would certainly die. But the latter prospect, Lincoln was convinced, was unlikely, particularly if Douglas, in the name of democracy, was permitted to pursue a course inimical to freedom.

After asserting this conviction, he turned back to 1854, when apparently the advance of slavery had been halted, to begin to marshal his evidence. Before the advent of popular sovereignty, he asserted, "... slavery [had been] excluded from more than half the States by State Constitutions, and from most of the national territory by Congressional prohibition" (II, 462); but the repeal of the Missouri Compromise had nullified those prohibitions, opening all the territories to slavery. That was the opening move, Lincoln asserted, in the attempt to pervert the meaning of democracy:

> This necessity had not been overlooked; but had been provided for, as well as might be, in the notable argument of *"squatter sovereignty,"* otherwise called *"sacred right of self-government,"* which latter prhase, though expressive of the only rightful basis of any government, was so perverted in this attempted use of it as to amount to just this: That if any *one* man choose to enslave *another,* no *third* man shall be allowed to object. (II, 462)

Lincoln proceeded to marshal the evidence pointing to that offensive: the Kansas-Nebraska Bill had been passed without a provision that slavery could be excluded by the people of the territories; the Dred Scott suit began its journey through the courts; Buchanan was elected after the decision was deferred and then, after his inauguration, endorsed that decision; under the Kansas-Nebraska Bill, Buchanan accepted the Lecompton Constitution, thus adding to the political power as well as geographic expansion of slavery.

These facts were irrefutable, but Lincoln had, thus far, excluded mention of Douglas from them. Then, deliberately striving for maximum effect in defining Douglas' role and beliefs while at the same time belittling his break with Buchanan, he turned to that point. He continued to refrain from referring to Douglas by name, but he made evident Douglas' role in slavery's advance into free territory:

> At length a squabble springs up between the President and the author of the Nebraska bill, on the *mere* question of *fact,* whether the Lecompton constitution was or was not, in any just sense, made by the people of Kansas; and in that squabble the latter declares that all he wants is a fair vote for the people, and that he *cares* not whether slavery be voted *down* or voted *up.* I do not understand his declaration that he cares not whether slavery be voted down or voted up, to be intended by him other than as an

apt definition of the *policy* he would impress upon the public
mind—the *principle* for which he declares he has suffered much,
and is ready to suffer to the end. (II, 463–64)

This point Lincoln stressed to the end; it was, he knew, the
only issue upon which Douglas' rejection of Buchanan and the
Lecompton Constitution could be made ignoble in the eyes of
those who had begun to see him as a champion of freedom. In
one sense, Lincoln was unfair to Douglas, ignoring the personal
and political courage that he displayed; but in another he was
scrupulously fair: Douglas had made the statement publicly, regardless of his own personal convictions; and he should be called
to account for it.

The rest of the evidence pointed toward implications of the
Dred Scott decision for the future—the expansion of slavery to
the Northern free states—and the duplicity of Buchanan—and
Douglas—in withholding their acceptance of that decision until
after the Democratic administration had safely come into power.
Under this alliance of political power seeking a dynastic succes-
sion and slavery seeking expansion, the call to action by the
Republicans, as Lincoln saw it, was clear: "To meet and over-
throw the power of that dynasty, is the work now before all those
who would prevent that consummation" (II, 467).

The first necessary step, he went on, was to stop the Douglas
movement in the ranks of the Republicans. A plot of the Douglas
Democrats, designed to rally misled Republicans and others to
his support, had to be exposed for what it was and Douglas for
what he supported rather than for what his supporters asserted
he believed: "They remind us that *he* is a very *great man* and
that the largest of *us* are very small ones. Let this be granted. But
'a *living dog* is better than a *dead lion.*' Judge Douglas, if not a
dead lion for *this work,* is at least a *caged* and *toothless* one. How
can he oppose the advances of slavery? He doesn't *care* anything
about it. His avowed *mission* is *impressing* the 'public heart' to
care nothing about it" (II, 467).

Even worse, Lincoln asserted, the revival of the African slave
trade was a logical result of the Douglas policies. If a revival of
that trade came about, he maintained, Douglas, who would allow
men to take slaves into the territories, could hardly refuse to let
them be purchased in the cheapest market. And this, he re-

minded his audience, was on the African coast. Property is property, Lincoln insisted that Douglas maintained; and, as an advocate of free trade, Douglas could hardly insist upon a protective tariff to prevent competition from imported African slaves in American markets.

Lincoln's conclusion was a plea for concerted action on the part of all who were dedicated to opposing the spread of slavery —action that excluded those, like Douglas, who had shown no such interest. Once action had begun, Lincoln promised, once the faith in freedom was accepted, there could be no doubt of the nature of the undivided nation of the future:

> Our cause, then, must be entrusted to, and conducted by its own undoubted friends—those whose hands are free, whose hearts are in the work—who *do care* for the result.
>
> Two years ago the Republicans of the nation mustered over thirteen hundred thousand strong.
>
> We did this under the single impulse of resistance to a common danger, with every external circumstance against us.
>
> Of *strange, discordant,* and even, *hostile* elements, we gathered from the four winds, and *formed* and fought the battle through, under the constant hot fire of a disciplined, proud, and pampered enemy.
>
> Did we brave all *then,* to *falter* now?—*now*—when that same enemy is *wavering,* dissevered and beligerent?
>
> The result is not doubtful. We shall not fail—if we stand firm, we shall not fail.
>
> *Wise councils* may *accelerate* or *mistakes delay* it, but sooner or later the victory is sure to come. (II, 468–69)

This speech is Lincoln's most remarkable of the decade, with the possible exception of the lost speech of two years before. More clearly than any other, it marked the synonymous political and moral paths that Lincoln was convinced the Republican party must take. Like the earlier speech and the Cooper Union address of 1860, Lincoln designed this speech to imprint his mark upon the party he had adopted and was determined to see triumph. His determination was not, however, as a matter of political power and right, but in the interest of the moral right that he asserted must prevail. Perhaps political rivalries influenced Lincoln's distrust of Douglas, but his prime motivation was moral. Douglas had not opposed the extension of slavery in the past, he was not doing so in the present, and there was no reason to expect him to do so in the future.

Equally remarkable is the fact that Lincoln did not attack Douglas personally in the speech, in spite of the obvious opportunity. Personal friendship, respect, and awareness of Douglas' personal distaste for slavery were undoubtedly partially responsible, as unquestionably was Lincoln's awareness that, if his strategy failed, he would have to make a political truce with Douglas. But not only was personal attack unnecessary, with Douglas' own words and the suggestion of a conspiracy with Buchanan and Chief Justice Roger B. Taney to damn him in any Republican gathering; but it is evident that Lincoln was done with personal attacks and with the savage satire with which he was accustomed to destroying political enemies. With his new faith, he had begun to find a new tolerance, based on his confidence in the ultimate triumph of good over evil, that led him to realize that human beings may differ, that they may be mistaken, but that their motives may be sincere and their integrity unquestionable. This, Lincoln knew, was certainly the case among men of good will North and South. From this time Lincoln's only interest was to destroy evil and to save men.

Actually, as Lincoln was well aware, his differences with Douglas were not so extreme as they seemed. Each sought a solution that would minimize strife over slavery in the nation, and each was determined that it should be done democratically, just as each recognized the constitutionality of slavery in spite of personal dislike for the institution. Sharing a mutual faith in the American Union, each, however, derived that faith from a different political tradition, one to which each turned for the answers to the problem of slavery and the preservation of the Union. Consequently, each found a different way to what was a mutual goal, and neither was able to accept that of the other; each saw in the other's program certain death for America and its freedom.

Douglas' tradition came from Jefferson and Jackson, and it was embodied in the Democratic party of his time; Lincoln's came from John Adams, Henry Clay, and, increasingly, Daniel Webster; and he sought to make it the philosophy of the Republicans. Douglas' concept of democracy included, as did Jefferson's, a belief in limited government, with the ultimate power residing in the citizens, who expressed their will, the will of the majority, through their state and local governments. Superimposed on this Jeffersonian basis were, for Douglas, two factors, both of them mystic rather than rational, that he derived from Jackson. The first was an unlimited faith in the common people to make the right decision through their intuitive understanding of the right. The second was a no-less-mystic reverence for the Union, in which the majority will of the people must also prevail. The logical means, therefore, for the solution of the slavery controversy, was to denationalize it through popular sovereignty. Made a local issue, it could never threaten the Union.

Lincoln inherited from Adams and the eighteenth century a recognition that government must be by reason rather than whim; and concurrent with this belief was a limited faith in the wisdom of the people and a real fear of the tyranny of the majority. From Clay, he derived his awareness of government as the means of insuring maximum freedom without license to abuse that of others. He acquired a reverence for a rule of law rather than of men; and he learned to seek, when necessary to protect freedom, to accept the rule of law, even when it was wrong, until it could be changed constitutionally. Superimposed on these early acceptances, and reviving the Jacksonian faith of his youth, was the late but powerful influence of Webster, whose replies to Hayne and Calhoun in the Senate gave Lincoln a reverence, no less mystic than Douglas', for the Union itself as the ultimate source of good in American life. Consequently, in his program Lincoln advocated constant political, moral, and legal pressure, within the framework of law, to limit and eventually exterminate slavery. Slavery could not be denationalized until it ceased to exist, Lincoln asserted; and he was determined to bring that end about.

Less democratic in an absolute sense than Douglas' position, rejecting as it did the right of the people to choose evil, it was at the same time more democratic in its insistence that no man had the right to extend his freedom at the expense of another. The right to property was, consequently, limited; there could be no property rights in human beings. Not an appeal to "higher law" or natural law, Lincoln's appeal was for logical, rational, humanistic definitions of democracy, freedom, and property in keeping with the ideals of his tradition.

Lincoln was not an Abolitionist in spite of his willingness to clothe his rational analysis of the problem in emotional terms. But never did he bring in the echo of the clang of chains or the terror of personalized slavery. Instead, he opposed the institution itself; and his attack was rationally developed, based in logic, in law, and in tradition rather than in the charged, personalized issues of the Abolitionists. But obvious in Lincoln's approach in the speech is a kinship to the revivalist oratorical tradition of the frontier evangelism of his youth. In the speech, Lincoln portrayed the devil, horrible and real; he pointed out his snares; he made clear the misconceptions and the search for the easy path, which would lead to undescribable horror unless avoided in time; and he concluded with a fervent plea for the faithful to join him, to pit their collective will against the servants of darkness, and to insure their own salvation in the process.

Certainly one of Lincoln's most effective speeches in a political meeting, it had both the immediate and long-term effects that Lincoln sought. Although the speech was called radical and inflammatory in some circles, it united the party effectively behind Lincoln, it brought in the waverers who had been tempted by Douglas, and it gave Lincoln's cause the attention it merited outside Illinois. As Lincoln moved into the campaign against Douglas, he was reasonably certain of success. He had carried the fight to Douglas, had put him in a position that demanded answers rather than equivocation; and in shrewd frontier fashion he had given Douglas his choice: he could placate the Illinois electorate in 1858 and alienate the South, or, in attempting to hold the South for 1860, endanger his re-election in Illinois. Douglas could neither escape the trap Lincoln had set for him nor find a politically expedient middle course.

Douglas did make the attempt to answer, believing that Lincoln's accusations were inflaming the crisis rather than permitting it to disappear as a national issue. He denied the implications of conspiracy between himself and Buchanan, Pierce, and Taney; he warned against the dangers of sectionalism that would, unless checked, drive the North and South further apart; he accused Lincoln of fomenting that sectionalism; and he called Lincoln's program to halt the extension of slavery mere Abolitionism. In all of these countercharges, Douglas had much evidence and logic in his support, but he could not evade what Lincoln declared was the central issue: the morality and justice of slavery. And Lincoln gave him no respite.

II *The Lincoln-Douglas Debates*

Finally, after a month of exchanges, Douglas, against his better judgment and his political instinct, agreed to a series of face-to-face encounters with Lincoln in towns and cities throughout Illinois. Douglas had little to gain; he was the incumbent; and his name was already known throughout Illinois and the nation, while Lincoln had little to lose. But, as the details were arranged, Douglas' constituents were confident, Lincoln's dubious.

The debates were to cover, as nearly as possible, the entire state, beginning at Ottawa on August 21. From there the debaters were to move to Freeport on August 27; Jonesboro, September 15; Charleston, September 18; Galesburg, October 7; Quincy, October 13; and Alton, October 15. Each candidate intended, between debates, to speak frequently and freely on the issues; and in the debates they agreed to alternate giving the opening speeches. Douglas, beginning at Ottawa, was to speak for an hour; Lincoln, to follow for an hour and a half; and Douglas, to close with half an hour's remarks. The pattern was then to be repeated, with Lincoln speaking first at Freeport, and then the two would continue to alternate throughout the series. Lincoln felt somewhat out-traded by the fact that Douglas would have four "openings" to his three, but that was a small concession; Douglas had made the major one; and the series was arranged.

The positions and charges presented by Lincoln and Douglas in their speeches prior to the debates during June and July—often with the other present in the audience or scheduled to speak the same or the next day—were largely those that provided the substance of the formal series. Douglas sought to justify his doctrine of popular sovereignty and to fasten upon Lincoln and the Republicans the names of Abolitionist and sectionalist; Lincoln emphasized his conviction that slavery could not be denationalized, that the country must become all slave or all free; and he sought to identify Douglas as a dupe or conspirator in the expansion of slavery. Douglas argued that the Dred Scott decision could be neither revoked nor appealed; Lincoln maintained that it was part of a Democratic conspiracy and that the Supreme Court could be forced to reverse itself. Douglas asserted that Lincoln sought national uniformity and regimentation;

Lincoln denied it, resurrecting the charges of conspiracy against Douglas with Pierce, Buchanan, and Taney, as he had in the "House Divided" speech. In the series of charges and counter-charges there was no clear-cut trend, but Lincoln felt that he had acquitted himself well in the preliminary exchange of four speeches, one by each, in Chicago on July 9 and 10 and in Springfield on July 17.

In the Chicago speeches, race became an issue between the two. Douglas was frank in asserting that he did not approve of Lincoln's reasons for the attacks on the Supreme Court—essentially, Douglas asserted, Lincoln was demanding equality for the Negro:

> He objects to it because that decision declared that a negro descended from African parents who were brought here and sold as slaves is not, and cannot be a citizen of the United States. He says it is wrong, because it deprives the negro of the benefits of that clause of the Constitution which says that citizens of one state shall enjoy all the privileges and immunities of the several states; in other words, he thinks it wrong because it deprives the negro of the privileges, immunities, and rights of citizenship, which pertain, according to that decision, only to the white man. I am free to say to you that in my opinion this government of ours is founded on the white basis. It was made by the white man, for the benefit of the white man, to be administered by white men, in such manner as they should determine. It is also true that a negro, an Indian, or any other man of an inferior race to a white man, should be permitted to enjoy, and humanity requires that he should have all the rights, privileges and immunities which he is capable of exercising consistent with the safety of society. I would give him every right and every privilege which his capacity would enable him to enjoy, consistent with the good of the society in which he lived. But you may ask me what are these rights and these privileges. My answer is that each state must decide for itself the nature and extent of these rights. Illinois has decided for itself . . .[1]

Douglas was not reflecting either personal bigotry or prejudice in his concept of racial superiority and inferiority or in the relationship between the Negro and society; he was reflecting both the spirit and the science of his age; and, indeed, in the context of the times his position was liberally humanitarian. He had straddled the issue, so that both Negrophobes and friends could find something to accept. But the ultimate definition of the Negro's place in society, he reiterated, was not for him to decide; it was entirely a state matter.

Douglas' assertion forced Lincoln to clarify his position, and he did so, like Douglas striking a balance within the context of the beliefs and scientific pronouncements of his age. But Lincoln's balance was in the direction of equality in the spirit of the Declaration of Independence rather than that of majority rule in a democracy:

> We were often—more than once at least—in the course of Judge Douglas' speech last night, reminded that this government was made for white men—that he believed it was made for white men. Well, that is putting it into a shape in which no one wants to deny it, but the Judge then goes into his passion for drawing inferences that are not warranted. I protest, now and forever, against that counterfeit logic which presumes that because I do not want a negro woman for a slave, I do necessarily want her for a wife. My understanding is that I need not have her for either, but as God made us separate, we can leave one another alone and do one another much good thereby.... The Judge regales us with the terrible enormities that take place by the mixture of the races; that the inferior race bears the superior down. Why, Judge, if we do not let them get together in the Territories they won't mix there. (II, 498)

Lincoln neither declared his personal point of view nor denied Douglas's assertion that he sought political equality for the Negro, a policy that Lincoln supported only through a war-inspired selective process. Instead, he saw the opportunity to turn Douglas' argument against him, and the point made was simple and obvious, yet profound: the evils of slavery, opposed by the Republicans, and the dangers of racial mixing, feared by Douglas Democrats, could be easily solved by preventing the expansion of slavery.

But, finally, Lincoln did not depend on semantic or linguistic gymnastics to make his point; instead, he turned to the source of the American ideal: "So I say in relation to the principle that all men are created equal, let it be as nearly reached as we can. If we cannot give freedom to every creature, let us do nothing that will impose slavery upon any other creature.... If we do not do so we are turning in the contrary direction, that our friend Judge Douglas proposes—not intentionally—as working in the traces tend to make this one universal slave nation" (II, 501). The ideal was, perhaps, unattainable; but to refuse to attempt to reach it was to Lincoln unthinkable; that course could result only in compounded evil.

It is evident that Lincoln did have the better of the exchange. Invariably, in debating the specific issues and general implications of slavery, he found himself turning instinctively to absolute standards rather than to political or social expediencies, to institutional and social perfectibility under law rather than the perpetuation of imperfections through the mandate of passion. And he insisted that the role of leadership, whether by a party or an individual, was to lead toward that perfection, however apparently unattainable, rather than to reflect the fancies, passions, and preferences of the moment. In this conviction Lincoln remained both puritan and son of the Enlightenment.

The Springfield speeches on July 17 were largely repetitious of the Chicago exchange. Douglas, in his attack against the "House Divided" theme and Lincoln's rejection of the Dred Scott decision, accused Lincoln of Abolitionism, anti-democratic principles, and advocating Negro equality. Lincoln denied the charges, raising once more the specter of slavery's dominating the nation. The issues had by this time become so highly charged emotionally that each attacked the other's programs in terms of the secret and open fears of the unknown and the unthinkable in spite of the determination of both men to base their positions on logical, rational grounds. Fears had, by this time, become so real that perhaps rational debate in a rational context had become impossible; nevertheless, in the formal series of debates, both were determined to try.

In many respects Illinois at the time was a microcosm of the nation. The northern tier of counties, settled largely by New Englanders, was almost solidly Republican; the southern tier drew much of its population from the border and slave states, and it was solidly Democratic; and the middle tier might go either way. Consequently, the strategy of each candidate took this distribution into account in planning the substance of speeches; and both knew that the crucial battle would be fought in the middle counties, where four of the speeches were scheduled. But telling blows could be struck and easy defenses erected through skillful use of the extremes.

Douglas, facing a hostile or indifferent audience at Ottawa, mounted his offensive immediately but with restraint; he spoke kindly of Lincoln while he supported his own record. But his attack rested upon the threat of Negro equality and upon Lincoln's opposition to the Dred Scott decision. At the end Douglas restated his faith in popular sovereignty, under which, he asserted, the Union would rise to new heights, while Lincoln's aims could only result in strife. Particularly evident is the suggestion, running through the speech, that Lincoln, from his opposition to the Mexican War to his opposition to the Dred Scott decision, had demonstrated what was ineptness at best, radicalism at worst.

Lincoln, in facing a friendly, sympathetic audience, did not hesitate to answer Douglas' charges, particularly on the issue of Negro equality, again attempting with considerable success to turn Douglas' accusations into an attack on him. But, in so doing, Lincoln elevated his own position in the debates to a moral level that he knew was impregnable:

> ... I have no purpose directly or indirectly to interfere with the institution of slavery in the States where it exists. I believe I have no lawful right to do so, and I have no inclination to do so. I have no purpose to introduce political and social equality between the white and the black races. There is a physical difference between the two, which in my judgement will probably forever forbid their living together upon the footing of perfect equality, and inasmuch as it becomes a necessity that there must be a difference, I, as well as Judge Douglas, am in favor of the race to which I belong, having the superior position. I have never said anything to the contrary, but I hold that notwithstanding all this, there is no reason in the world why the negro is not entitled to all the natural rights enumerated in the Declaration of Independence, the right to life, liberty, and the pursuit of happiness, I hold that he is as much entitled to these as the white man. I agree with Judge Douglas that he is not my equal in many respects—certainly not in color, perhaps not in moral or intellectual endowment. But in the right to eat the bread, without leave of any body else, which his own hand earns, *he is my equal and the equal of Judge Douglas, and the equal of every living man.* (III, 16)

In much of Lincoln's speech, even temper and a good deal of humor prevailed, setting both the tone and the subject of his portion of the debates; and, in spite of questions and demanded answers, answers and counterquestions, little that was new was added to the controversy. The issues had been clearly drawn, and the only resolution could be at the ballot box—as both contestants knew. Douglas attempted to pin Lincoln down at Ottawa with a series of questions designed to trap Lincoln into assertions that he placed emancipation above country and hence was nothing but an Abolitionist, but Lincoln evaded them to counterattack at Freeport.

The ensuing counterquestions have attracted the most speculation and commentary of any in the debates because out of them came what became known as Douglas' Freeport Doctrine, a statement that led to denunciation of Douglas in the South. This counterquestion was the only truly calculated risk of the campaign, as Lincoln was aware. The crucial question was the second of a list of four, a question easily and satisfactorily answerable by Douglas within the context of the senatorial campaign but with implications beyond the borders of Illinois. Warned against asking it, Lincoln determined to take the risk, and he did, demanding that Douglas answer: "Can the people of a United States Territory, in any lawful way, against the wishes of any citizen of the United States, exclude slavery from its limits prior to the formation of a State Constitution?" (III, 43).

Here was the crux of popular sovereignty, as Lincoln saw it; and that crux was its inherent weakness. No answer satisfactory to all the people could be found. If Douglas replied *yes*, he would attract much still-doubtful support in Illinois, perhaps enough to insure his re-election; but it would be at the price of denying the Dred Scott decision, which he accepted as the law of the land. At the same time, he would make impossible a united national Democratic party under his leadership. If, on the other hand, he said *no*, he would lose Illinois and the election. Douglas, for once, would be pinned on the dilemma at the heart of his doctrine: slavery would not be denationalized because the country would not permit it to be. No matter how popular or unpopular the institution might be in one or the other sections or states, it was an issue of national concern; and the opposing fears raised by it were, however illogical, nevertheless real. Douglas' answer would reinforce those fears, either in the North, denying him the senatorship, or in the South, denying him a unified party. In either case, the answer would deny him the Presidency.

Douglas' reply was direct; it was the logical culmination of popular sovereignty, it was satisfactory to Illinois, but it alienated the South, which had found its justification in the Dred Scott decision:

> . . . he has no excuse for pretending to be in doubt as to my position on that question. It matters not what way the Supreme Court may hereafter decide as to the abstract question whether slavery may or may not go into a territory under the Constitution, the people have the lawful means to introduce it or exclude it as they please, for the reason that slavery cannot exist a day or an hour anywhere, unless it is supported by local police regulations. Those police regulations can only be established by the local legislature, and if the people are opposed to slavery they will elect representatives to that body who will by unfriendly legislation effectually prevent the introduction of it into their midst. If, on the contrary, they are for it, their legislation will favor its extension. Hence, no matter what the decision of the Supreme Court may be on that abstract question, still the right of the people to make a slave territory or a free territory is perfect and complete under the Nebraska Bill. I hope Mr. Lincoln deems my answer satisfactory on that point.[2]

The question and its answer provided much of the substance of the following debates, and it is evident that Lincoln found the answer to his satisfaction, although not for the reason that Douglas expected. There is no reason to question Douglas' sincerity in his answer; on the contrary, he was painfully honest, going far beyond what he might have said in pointing out how the ultimate will of the people might make itself felt. Nor is there evidence to suggest that Douglas was unaware of the political repercussions of the speech North and South, nor that he was merely playing to a Northern audience. And in his answer he made inevitable the split in the Democratic party that he and others had labored to prevent for a decade.

The series of debates provided a colorful, dramatic show in the finest nineteenth-century American political tradition: cannons boomed, flags waved, brass bands played, and the audiences enjoyed the spectacle, venting their partisan feelings freely or waiting skeptically to be convinced. And on November 2, 1858, they went to the polls to determine in the public mind the immediate winner in the terms from which Douglas' policy took its validity and its meaning. But the collective voice to which Douglas ascribed innate wisdom was muted. Four thousand more Republican than Douglas Democratic votes were cast, but the Buchanan Democrats had polled more than five thousand, making, in effect, the Republican total a plurality rather than a majority. And the structure of the new legislature insured Douglas' victory by a majority of eight. However, Douglas' fifty-four final votes constituted considerably less than a mandate; Lincoln had fought the "Little Giant" almost to a standstill with forty-four.

Both the speeches and the issues have largely been lost in the drama of the debates and their aftermath. A clear-cut victory for either man was out of the question in terms of political results or the qualities of the speeches themselves. On balance, however, it appears that Lincoln's questioning technique gave him the best of the exchange. Not only did he turn psychological and political handicaps imposed on him by Douglas into offensive advantages, but he forced Douglas to debate on his terms on the Freeport issue. Simply by fighting Douglas to a standstill on other issues, he made a national reputation as a shrewd, skillful spokesman for the Republican cause, preventing a future connection between Douglas and the Republicans. The issues, as Lincoln defined them, were too clear to allow that; and Douglas was forced to become a leader not of the Democratic party but of a faction of a seriously damaged party.

The issues in the debate went far beyond those concerned with the expansion or limitation of slavery as new territories and states sought admission into the union. This aspect of the debate was merely one manifestation of a much deeper disagreement, as Lincoln knew when he advanced his "House Divided" thesis. Ultimately, the issue was not the legality of slavery but the morality of it; and Lincoln determined to keep the debate on a moral plane and to force Douglas to join him there, which Douglas did in his pronouncement of the Freeport Doctrine. In asserting that slavery could not exist in a territory without the consent of its residents, Douglas made clear that ultimately Lincoln's position was correct: the legality or constitutionality of an institution was meaningless without moral sanction. And, as

Lincoln reiterated, the American morality, as set forth in the Declaration of Independence, did not equivocate; all men were, in its terms, created equal, and to deny that equality through narrow laws or interpretations of laws was to stand exposed as corrupt. Legality and constitutionality might change—indeed, they had to change; but the American ideal remained unchanging.

Lincoln's concept of racial equality was controlled by social practicality. Like Douglas, he did not accept the principle of absolute equality in all things. But Douglas asserted that he did not care about the Negro's lot; that the white people of the various localities had the inherent right to determine it. Lincoln, however, continually asserted that he did care; that in the fundamental right to control his destinies and to receive the fruits of his labor, the Negro was the equal of any white man. The Declaration of Independence, unqualified, was to Lincoln a universal human document rather than a white one.

The immediate practical solutions advanced by the two men were not so far apart as was assumed. Lincoln's advocacy of the limitation of slavery, while permitting it to exist in states already slave, would have the same immediate effect as Douglas' doctrine of popular sovereignty as defined at Freeport: the existence and the denial of slavery in the same country at the same time. But the long-term implications were drastically different; Lincoln saw his position as prefatory to the eventual disappearance of slavery, in keeping with the Declaration of Independence; but Douglas regarded his as a final solution, one that Lincoln held was impossible.

The true significance of the debates lies in the fact that it was a decisive discussion. The questions raised were fundamental: Should the slavery problem be local or national? Is the institution democratic or undemocratic? Can the issue be solved by compromise? In defining his position, Douglas was certain; his solution was, he was convinced, democratic. But, as Lincoln continually pointed out, at its core it was not; it was a denial of the natural rights tradition upon which the concept of democracy itself was based. Lincoln, with the clarity of his insight into the problem, knew, however, that no decision was possible in terms of practical democratic processes evolved by Jefferson and Jackson. The entire nation, as he saw it, must regard the institution in terms of the natural rights of man; and in those terms, it must decide what it will be, democratic or undemocratic; to be both at once was impossible.

In defining the questions Lincoln sought a national rather than local definition of the word "democracy," and he made clear the weakness inherent in popular sovereignty and the limitations of majority rule, the practical guideline of a Jacksonian era. In forcing Douglas to join him in making that definition, Lincoln focused national attention on the issue underlying the entire institution of slavery: slavery and democracy are, by definition, incompatible; and the nation must choose national slavery without democracy or national democracy without slavery. To Lincoln's mind, there was no other possibility.

This clarity of insight led Lincoln directly to the Presidency. Combined with his mystic concept of the Union as the greatest good, he believed in the tradition of Jefferson and Jackson that democracy must be the national value, that there could be no Union without democracy, but that democracy itself was impossible without the Union. An article of faith as well as a logical deduction from the heritage of the eighteenth century, this belief led to his conclusion that, above all, the Union must be preserved. And that conclusion led to war.

In Lincoln's development as a writer, the speeches of the campaign of 1858 were of less significance than they were to his political career or to the future of the nation. Although he was dealing with a problem more emotional than rational in its effect upon his listeners and readers, he attempted to lay a rational base for each of his assertions and questions. Consequently, rationality and logic provide the framework of each of the speeches, even in his definitions of the nature of equality. The speeches, too, are clothed in an atmosphere of coolness, of tolerance, of common sense. But, in spite of these techniques—the product of his development through the years—there is an emotional fervor, an air of moral earnestness and conviction new to his technique, that transcends all the logical argument he marshals in the documents. Lincoln was not, in the speeches, appealing to his audience to think; he was appealing to them to have faith.

In the style that he had developed through the years, the speeches are starkly functional, spiced by occasional flourishes of wit, but almost entirely phrased in the language of living speech. It is an honest style, blunt and direct, and unrhetorical in the nineteenth-century fashion. Deliberate in its movement toward carefully defined points, Lincoln's style is, at times, almost ponderous, depending for its force upon the fire of delivery as well as upon the power of his argument. Almost invariably at the end of his speeches in the debates, he posed a final challenge, a final question, that focused the attention of his audience upon the ultimate impossibility of an easy solution; and he defied Douglas to respond. But increasingly, in the conclusion of the concurrent speeches not part of the debates and occasionally in the debate speeches themselves, Lincoln's appeal for faith was direct.

III   The Coming Explosion

Although defeated in the election, Lincoln was confident rather than disheartened. He was convinced that the Republican cause was just and that the Douglas proposals would not work. His correspondence during the ensuing months was full of confidence in the justice and ultimate prevalence of the cause. Because of that cause, he knew that his own predicament as a defeated candidate whose law practice had deteriorated during the contest was unimportant. On November 19, he appealed to Henry Asburgy for faith: ".... The fight must go on. The cause of civil liberty must not be surrendered at the end of *one*, or even, one *hundred* defeats. Douglas had the ingenuity to be supported in the late contest both as the best means to *break down*, and to *uphold* the Slave interest. No ingenuity can keep those antagonistic elements in harmony long. Another explosion will come soon" (III, 336).

To Dr. Anson G. Henry, he was more explicit in describing his personal predicament, but he remained confident that the contest had been worthwhile in view of its signficance: "I am glad I made the late race. It gave me a hearing on the great and durable question of the age, which I could have had in no other way; and though I now sink out of view, and shall be forgotten, I believe I have made some marks which will tell for the cause of civil liberty long after I am gone" (III, 336).

Right and wrong in his assessment of the effects of the debates

—right in his view of the signficance of the problem and the coming explosion and wrong in his view of his own future— Lincoln prepared to pass into obscurity; for a seat in the Senate, after two defeats, was out of his reach. Both the party's finances and his own were in chaos; and, determined to reorder both as quickly as possible, he began to solicit for the party while returning to his law practice. It began to appear that he and the Illinois Central Railroad determined that his future would consist of a long, close, profitable arrangement.

But neither the issue of slavery nor Lincoln's role in the party opposed to it would disappear. The campaign had enhanced his reputation outside Illinois, and he was invited to speak throughout that state and in others. And in the background a morally righteous Abolitionist named John Brown, at once a hero and a criminal in the warfare of bleeding Kansas, was gathering together a small group, gaining support and encouragement, and preparing to establish himself in a Maryland farmhouse. The explosion was, as Lincoln had predicted, at hand.

"... let us ... dare to do our duty ..."

IN LINCOLN'S closing remarks at the final debate at Alton, Illinois, on October 15, 1858, he defined the issue that would dominate his political actions, thinking, and writing during the next two years; and he made clear the theme that would underlie his examination of the problem that, he said, would continue "... when these poor tongues of Judge Douglas and myself shall be silent" (III, 315): "It is the eternal struggle between these two principles—right and wrong—throughout the world. They are the two principles that have stood face to face from the beginning of time; and will ever continue to struggle. The one is the common right of humanity and the other the divine right of kings" (III, 315).

Throughout 1859 and 1860, in spite of the demands of his personal and professional life, Lincoln continued to speak out. Invited to Kansas to speak, he wrote on March 4, 1859, that "It will push me hard to get there without injury to my own business" (III, 371), but in December he was there. In August he spoke in Council Bluffs, Iowa. The text has been lost, but the Democratic Council Bluffs *Eagle* heard it as "... a lengthy and ingenious analysis of the Nigger question..." in which he proclaimed that "... he was willing to run for president in 1860, a Southern man with Northern principles, or in other words, with Abolition proclivities." All in all, the account concluded, "He was listened to with much attention, for his Waterloo defeat by Douglas has magnified him into quite a hero here."[1]

I *The Ohio Speeches of 1859*

In September Lincoln was in Ohio, invited by the Republicans of that state to oppose the appearance of Douglas in the fall election that would elect a state legislature which would, in turn, elect a United States Senator. The election was crucial in Ohio, and it had strong implications for the Presidential election the next year; so Lincoln, who had never before made a political speech in Ohio and was little known there, consented to go. The resulting series of speeches by the two men, although from different platforms on different days, was, in effect a continuation of the previous year's debates and a foreshadowing of the conflict of the next, as the carnival atmosphere seemed to anticipate.

Douglas, who had published a definitive article on his position in *Harper's Magazine* for September, spoke in Columbus on September 7, at Cincinnati on September 9, and at Wooster on September 16. Lincoln was to speak in Columbus on September 16 and at Dayton, Hamilton, and Cincinnati on September 17. The line of battle was as it had been the previous year, but the point of departure was the essay by Douglas published in *Harper's*. Its title was "The Dividing Line Between Federal and Local Authority," subtitled "Popular Sovereignty in the Territories." An attack on Seward's concept of the irrepressible conflict and Lincoln's "House Divided" thesis without mentioning either of them by name, it was an extended argument for popular soverignty as the only means of preventing the tragedy he insisted would result if those concepts became widespread.

In the essay Douglas attempted, as his thesis sentence implied, "... to mark distinctly the dividing line between Federal and Local authority."[2] The result was a *tour de force* in which Douglas examined the constitutional aspects and implications of the separate jurisdictions of the two authorities, Supreme Court pronouncements on the same issue, and, finally, the debates in Congress over the Kansas-Nebraska Act. His conclusion was, in keeping with his doctrine, a declaration for popular sovereignty: "The principle, under our political system, is *that every distinct political community, loyal to the Constitution and the Union, is entitled to all the rights, privileges, and immunities of self-government in respect to their local concerns and internal policy, subject only to the Constitution of the United States.*"[3]

The essay received much attention and acclaim, and Douglas' speeches in Ohio reiterated its arguments. His appearance in Ohio was a calculated risk by the Democrats as the breach between Douglas and Buchanan continued, but his reception was enthusiastic. And the Ohio Democrats were pleased with the result, a series of attacks on Lincoln, on Seward, and, to the delight of his audiences, on Governor Salmon P. Chase, who was to be Ohio's candidate for the Republican Presidential nomination in 1860. But Douglas did not heal Democratic wounds.

Lincoln used the *Harper's* essay as the focal point of his attack, and at Columbus he turned to a distinction between Douglas' concept of popular sovereignty, as set forth in the essay, and a true popular sovereignty. Again, the distinction was moral and ethical rather than political:

> I believe there is a genuine popular sovereignty. I think a definition of genuine popular sovereignty, in the abstract, would be about this: That each man shall do precisely as he pleases with himself and with all those things which exclusively concern him. Applied to government, this principle would be that a general government shall do all those things which pertain to it, and all the local governments shall do precisely as they please in respect to those matters which exclusively concern them. I understand that this government of the United States, under which we live, is based upon this principle; and I am misunderstood if it is supposed that I have any war to make upon that principle. (III, 405)

Lincoln's definition of popular sovereignty as he believed it to be was, as nearly as he could make it, a translation into American political terms of the biblical distinction between the realms of Caesar and of God, a political morality carefully defined. But he asserted that Douglas' concept would result not in delineations of responsibility but in oppression:

> Now, what is Judge Douglas's popular sovereignty? It is, as a principle, no other than that if one man chooses to make a slave of another man, neither that other man nor anybody else has a right to object. Applied in government, as he seeks to apply it, it is this: If, in a new Territory into which a few people are beginning to enter for the purpose of making their homes, they choose to either exclude slavery from their limits or to establish it there, however one or the other may affect the persons to be enslaved, or the infinitely greater number of persons who are afterward to inhabit that Territory, or the other members of the families of communities of which they are but an incipient member, or the general head of the family of States as parent of all— however their action may affect one or the other of these, there is

no power or right to interfere. That is Douglas' popular sovereignty applied. (III, 405)

The denationalization of slavery was impossible, Lincoln continued to maintain; its very nature and the nature of the country itself made it of national concern; and the only possible result of Douglas' unwillingness to admit that fact would be the steady, inevitable advance of slavery. Eventually, he predicted, that policy would result in the disappearance of the national heritage of freedom. In conclusion, he turned again to the moral issue at stake; and he contrasted it sharply with the doctrine advocated by Douglas:

> I ask attention to the fact that in a pre-eminent degree these popular sovereigns are at this work: blowing out the moral lights around us; teaching that the negro is no longer a man but a brute, that the Declaration has nothing to do with him, that he ranks with the crocodile and the reptile, that man, with body and soul, is a matter of dollars and cents. I suggest to this portion of the Ohio Republicans, or Democrats if there be any present, the serious consideration of this fact that there is now going on among you a steady process of debauching public opinion on this subject. (III, 425)

Lincoln's ironic play on the word "sovereigns" is delightful and deliberate, and it emphasizes his fear of the tyranny inherent in Douglas' position. Emphatically, Lincoln points out the mockery inherent in the pro-slavery position. In the slave supporter's insistence upon his rights under the democratic process, he denied the very basis of democracy itself and became more tyrannical than the last sovereign to claim domination over Americans. And the Declaration of Independence, a universal document, forever refuted such sovereignty.

At Cincinnati, on the edge of the slavocracy, Lincoln changed his approach. He dwelt on the narrowness of the river that separated slave state from free and then advanced the possibility that slavery, not a condition of race but of circumstances, might be extended from Negro to white. In ostensibly speaking not to Ohioans but to his fellow Kentuckians, he made his point clear: Douglas and the Democrats were apparently the friends of the South; but in reality, as the Freeport Doctrine made clear, their instability, inconclusiveness, and lack of foresight made them dangerous to everybody. Perhaps to still charges of sectionalism, but more likely because Lincoln as a Kentuckian believed it necessary, he spoke bluntly to the South:

> There are plenty of men in the slave States that are altogether good enough for me to be either President or Vice-President, provided they will profess their sympathy with our purpose and will place themselves on the ground that our men, upon principle, can vote for them. There are scores of them, good men in their character for intelligence and talent and integrity. If such a one will place himself upon the right ground, I am for his occupying one place upon the next Republican or Opposition ticket. I will heartily go for him. But unless he does so place himself, I think it a matter of perfect nonsense to attempt to bring about a union on any other basis. . . . The good old maxims of the Bible are applicable, and truly applicable, to human affairs, and in this, as in other things, we may say here that he who is not for us is against us; he who gathereth not with us, scattereth. (III, 461–62)

The appeal was made, but its import was clear: there would be no surrender and no compromise of principles. Lincoln held out the olive branch, but he made its acceptance conditional upon the acceptance with it of a national definition of Union, freedom, and democracy. Upon that ground he insisted that there be no confusion, ambiguity, or misunderstanding.

Although it is difficult to assess Lincoln's influence upon the Republican victory in the October elections—Chase, a radical Republican and outspoken Abolitionist was cool to Lincoln, whom he saw as too conservative and as a potential rival for the 1860 nomination, and the state had already declared its Republican sympathies by giving its electoral vote to Fremont in 1856—the effect on Lincoln's political fortunes was considerable. He spoke vigorously but conducted himself circumspectly, and his stature as a party regular and spokesman was enhanced. Not only did he continue the Republican emphasis upon the issues and advance his national reputation, but the nomination the next year was to be decided in Lincoln's favor by the Ohio delegation.

In his Ohio speeches and in those that followed, in Indianapolis on the way home and before the Wisconsin State Agricultural Society on September 30, Lincoln gave important clues to the rationale behind his constant emphasis upon equality of opportunity. In a portion of the Cincinnati speech apparently not used, he became personally reminiscent in a way he had never before associated with the issue:

> We know, Southern men declare that their slaves are better off than hired laborers amongst us. How little they *know,* whereof they speak! There is no permanent class of hired laborers amongst us. Twentyfive years ago, I was a hired laborer. The hired laborer of yesterday, labors on his own account today; and will hire others to labor for him to-morrow. Advancement—improvement in condition—is the order of things in a society of equals. . . .
> Free labor has the inspiration of hope; pure slavery has no hope. . . . (III, 462)

In Milwaukee on September 30, he carried on this theme, in abstract rather than personal terms, distinguishing between the "mud-sill" theory of labor and the "free labor" theory. His "mud-sill" theory concluded ". . . that all laborers are necessarily either *hired* laborers, or *slaves.* They further assume that whoever is a *hired* laborer, is fatally fixed in that condition for life. . . ." (III, 477–78). The free-labor theory was the foundation of education and the open society; it demanded that both be open to all. In his concluding remarks, he passed on from demanding a society of free labor to a vision of the future: "Let us hope . . . that by the best cultivation of the physical world, beneath and around us; and the intellectual and moral world within us, we shall secure an individual, social, and political prosperity and happiness, whose course shall be onward and upward, and which, while the earth endures, shall not pass away" (III, 482).

The first of these speeches was in a political context, in the heat of partisan debate; and the latter was carefully non-political; but the logical pattern is obvious, as is Lincoln's relationship to that pattern. The frontier itself was a denial of the "mud-sill" theory of labor; and even in the restlessness of Thomas Lincoln there was hope as he moved from Kentucky to Indiana to Illinois. But in the next generation the hope moved toward fulfillment as his son advanced from laborer to legislator to lawyer to congressman to nationally prominent politician. There could be no mistake in the implications, Lincoln knew; for he had seen hard work, when combined with self-education, determination, and enterprise, rewarded in his own case. But such advancement could come only in an open society.

Lincoln neither saw nor anticipated the rigidity of an industrial and economic system already limiting the advancement and mobility of many individuals; but if he had, believing as he did that labor was superior to capital, he might have modified the certainty with which he spoke. But the fact remains clear; he recognized that there was a difference between himself and his stepbrother, John D. Johnston, and it was not laziness. It was, he knew, an innate insight that Johnston lacked and that he himself had unsuccessfully attempted to supply him. But there is no question that Lincoln would have denounced the industrial system of the late nineteenth century as vehemently as he did the slave system had he perceived that it refused to permit or to support an open society. Lincoln, in his vision of the perfect society, saw Thomas Jefferson's democracy as he had himself experienced it; and he would settle for no less for others.

Lincoln's other speeches on the Wisconsin trip and later in Kansas were primarily political, but the conviction with which he supported a free and open society makes obvious the fact that he saw the society advocated by the South and acquiesced in by Douglas not merely as a political threat but as a denial of the meaning of his own life. In his opposition to the proposal advanced by Douglas as democratic in the Jeffersonian and Jacksonian tradition, Lincoln was strengthened by his knowledge from his own experience that Douglas was wrong and that the logical conclusion to the policies advocated by both of those great Democrats was the free society that he sought.

In December Lincoln sent to Jesse Fell, in response to a request, a brief biographical sketch containing a carefully objective description of himself. Consequently, on the verge of 1860, a year that Fell anticipated to be decisive, Lincoln's life was, in his own words, the American reality as he saw it and as he demanded that it be extended to all. Attached was a brief, vivid physical description, the only one Lincoln ever wrote: ". . . I am, in height, six feet, four inches, nearly; lean in flesh, weighing, on an average, one hundred and eighty pounds; dark complexion, with coarse black hair, and gray eyes—no other marks or brands recollected" (III, 512).

II *The Cooper Union Address*

With the only marks or brands not seen by himself—the mark
of the West and the brand of the incisive, relentless debater
on him—Lincoln went east to speak in New York and New
England two months later. He went under the shadow of the
explosion that he had foreseen. On October 16 John Brown and
his twenty-one followers had crossed the Potomac from their
farmhouse in Maryland to the Virginia arsenal town of Harper's
Ferry with the avowed intention of freeing the slaves and of
setting up an independent slave refuge in the mountains. After
capturing the arsenal, they settled down in it; and, after a siege,
they were captured by United States Marines under Colonel
Robert E. Lee. Tried in nearby Charleston for treason and murder, Brown was found guilty; and on December 2, he was
hanged, thereby achieving the martyrdom that he sought. But
the repercussions, like his spirit, went on in the North and the
South, engendering savage pleasure and fear among the extrem-
ists of the two sections while they embarrassed Lincoln and the
Republicans.

In Kansas, Lincoln first attempted to dispel that embarrassment. Brown had, a few years earlier, contributed his share of
blood to that bleeding area; and the Harper's Ferry raid, Lincoln
said, was both illegal and futile. Even though Brown was right
in thinking slavery wrong, Lincoln said, "That cannot excuse
violence, bloodshed, and treason" (III, 502). But the shadow of
Brown and an even greater explosion to come worried him; and,
drawing inspiration both from Brown and from Daniel Webster's
speeches of almost a decade before, he closed his Kansas speech
with a warning: "So, if constitutionally we elect a President, and
therefore you undertake to destroy the Union, it will be our duty
to deal with you as old John Brown has been dealt with. We
shall try to do our duty. We hope and believe that in no section
will a majority so act as to render such extreme measures necessary" (III, 502).

But, as Lincoln went East, he knew that the ghost of John
Brown would not be laid; Southern fears had not been allayed,
nor had the threats been refuted. If a Republican were elected
President, the South asserted that it would have no choice; the
contract among the states would be broken, and it would be

forced to seek its own destiny. And, Lincoln knew, his name was being associated with increasing frequency with the Republican nomination. His invitation to speak in New York had originally asked him to lecture at the Brooklyn Plymouth Church, whose pastor, the Reverend Henry Ward Beecher, was himself a celebrated speaker. When Lincoln had suggested that he speak on politics, the arrangements committee agreed. However, unknown to Lincoln, sponsorship of the lecture had been taken over by a group of Republicans determined to stop Seward's drive for the nomination, and they wanted to inspect Lincoln as a potential candidate. The site of the lecture was transferred to the Cooper Union in New York.

Aware that the lecture was a major opportunity, acutely conscious of his Western accent and mannerisms and of his awkward appearance, Lincoln prepared carefully by checking the historical evidence for his position and by re-examining the history of constitutional debate and legislation. He knew that his arguments, again attacking Douglas on slavery, were sound; but he was apparently nervous as he began his speech, aware that it was his maximum effort and that it was crucial to his own fortune and perhaps to that of his party.

Lincoln took as his thesis a statement from Douglas' speech the previous fall in Columbus. A statement with which there could be no disagreement in essence but many in interpretations, it contained the rationales advanced for popular sovereignty, for the abolition of slavery, for its expansion, and for its limitation. Lincoln quoted Douglas precisely: *"Our fathers, when they framed the Constitution under which we live, understood this question just as well, and even better, than we do now."* But, he asked, *"What was the understanding those fathers had of the question mentioned?"* (III, 522).

In the first part of the speech Lincoln provided the answer to that question, and the evidence he presented was impressive: of the thirty-nine signers of the Constitution, twenty-three, together with all seventy-six members of Congress, those who had approved the Bill of Rights, had clearly indicated that "... in their understanding, no line dividing local from federal authority, nor anything else, properly forbade the Federal Government to control as to slavery in federal territory" (III, 525). Proof of this interpretation, he asserted, was evident in their recorded actions:

the passage of the Northwest Ordinance of 1787, in which slavery was forbidden in the Old Northwest; the legislation passed
by the first Congress in 1789 to enforce that ordinance; the Territorial Act for Louisiana in 1804, which did not forbid but carefully controlled slavery in that newly annexed area; and finally
the Missouri Compromise of 1820, which drew a line beyond
which slavery was forbidden.

In each case, Lincoln maintained, some of that original thirty-
nine, a total of twenty-three, had by their votes, clearly indicated
their belief that Congress had the power to control or forbid
slavery in the territories. These men, Lincoln asserted, were
those who, in Douglas' words, "... framed the Government under
which we live" (III, 530). And the first Congress, in passing at
the same time the Bill of Rights and the Northwest Ordinance,
had verified their judgement. This evidence, for Lincoln, was
conclusive:

> But enough! *Let all those who believe that "our fathers, who
> framed the Government under which we live," understood this
> question just as well, and even better, than we do now," speak
> as they spoke, and act as they acted upon it. That is all Repub-.
> licans ask—all Republicans desire—in relation to slavery. As those
> fathers marked it, so let it be marked again, as an evil not to be
> extended, but to be tolerated and protected only because of and
> so far as its actual presence among us makes that toleration and
> protection a necessity. Let all the guaranties those fathers gave
> it, be, not grudgingly, but fully and fairly maintained.* For this
> Republicans contend, and with this, so far as I know or believe,
> they will be content. (III, 535)

In this part of the speech, Lincoln was the dispassionate trial
lawyer, looking for evidence in precedent and in documentary
fact. Without ambiguity or emotion, he recited those facts, emphasizing that the intent of the founding fathers, revealed in
their understanding of the relationship between state and federal
power, was not a matter for speculation or for wishful thinking.
It was, he demonstrated, a matter of record that could not be
denied. In that record, he found his authorization for the limitation of slavery as the foundation upon which his Republicanism stood.

In the second part, Lincoln addressed the South, using an approach that he had tested earlier in Cincinnati and Kansas. In

this part, he, like Daniel Webster at the beginning of the decade, examined Southern grievances and accusations, not, however, those against the North as a section, which Webster had largely dismissed while accepting the Fugitive Slave law, but those directed at the Republican party. As in the past, he began on the defensive, and followed the pattern he had used before to turn each accusation into a counteraccusation against its originators. In every case, he insisted, as in a court of law, the burden of the proof was on the accusers; and, not only had they failed to produce that proof, but often the available evidence proved the opposite. The first of these was the accusation that the Republicans were a sectional party:

> . . . We deny it. That makes an issue; and the burden of proof is on you. You produce your proof; and what is it? Why, that our party has no existence in your section—gets no votes in your section. The fact is substantially true; but does it prove the issue? If it does, then in case we should, without change of principle, begin to get votes in your section, we should thereby cease to be sectional. You cannot escape this conclusion; and yet, are you willing to abide by it? . . . The fact that we get no votes in your section, is a fact of your making and not of ours. . . . (III, 536)

The second charge—that of Republican radicalism—was, after his introductory examination of the facts demonstrating the attitude of the founding fathers, easy for Lincoln to refute:

> But you say you are conservative—eminently conservative—while we are revolutionary, destructive, or something of the sort. What is conservatism? Is it not adherence to the old and tried, against the new and untried? We stick to, contend for, the identical old policy on the point in controversey which was adopted by "our fathers who framed the Government under which we live;" while you with one accord reject, and scout, and spit upon that old policy, and insist upon substituting something new. . . . (III, 537)

The third accusation—that the Republicans insisted upon intensifying the controversy—was, in the light of the John Brown raid, more persistent and potentially more dangerous; and it was more difficult to deal with. Lincoln chose to treat it as two accusations: first, that the Republicans had made the slavery issue more prominent; second, that they stirred up slave insurrections.

The first he denied, insisting that the aggressive expansion of slavery had created the issue, and the second he rejected for lack of proof, indignantly threatening as he would in a courtroom:

> ... John Brown was no Republican, and you have failed to implicate a single Republican in his Harper's Ferry enterprise. If any member of our party is guilty in that matter, you know it or you do not know it. If you do know it, you are inexcusable for not designating the man and proving the fact. If you do not know it, you are inexcusable for asserting it, and especially for persisting in the assertion after you have tried and failed to make the proof. You need not be told that persisting in a charge which one does not know to be true, is simply malicious slander. (III, 538)

The accusations, as Lincoln examined them, were dismissed as distortions or without foundation; and he turned then briefly to the Republican position as he saw it: the power of emancipation, he asserted, was in the slaveholding states themselves; and he did not propose to tamper with it. But the power of limiting the expansion of slavery was a federal matter. Hence, he asserted, federal power had to be employed as the means whereby Southern fears could be prevented from becoming national fears and to assure "... that a slave insurrection shall never occur on any American soil which is now free from slavery" (III, 541).

Then he turned to the Republican accusations against the South: he asserted that, when the Southerners attempted to destroy Republicanism through their accusations, they at the same time threatened the country itself: "Your purpose, then, plainly stated, is that you will destroy the Government, unless you be allowed to construe and enforce the Constitution as you please, on all points in dispute between you and us. You will rule or ruin in all events" (III, 543).

The evidence, he pointed out, supported his contention; the South rather than the North had distorted the belief and intent of the founding fathers; and then it sought to escape the guilt for the effects of the resulting conflict:

> Under all these circumstances, do you really feel yourselves justified to break up this government, unless such a court decision as yours is, shall be at once submitted to as a conclusive and final rule of political action? But you will not abide the election of a

Republican President! In that supposed event, you say, you will destroy the Union; and then, you say, the great crime of having destroyed it will be on us! That is cool. A highwayman holds a pistol to my ear, and mutters through his teeth, "Stand and deliver, or I shall kill you, and then you shall be a murderer!" (III, 546–47)

In this part of the speech Lincoln held out no olive branch as he had in the past; instead, he was determined to make the Southerners see the illogicality of their position in terms of the harsh results which they had refused to recognize or consider. Lincoln was, he was convinced, dealing in reality—the kind with which he had been familiar all his life; and in his bluntly graphic words he determined to make the South understand that reality with its minds and feel it in its bones. Nothing, he felt, could be more dangerously misleading than to ignore the implications of rash words or actions.

In his final words Lincoln turned to his fellow Republicans, pleading for the same rationality and calmness which he admonished the South to show, as he pointed out the course they must take: "... *It is exceedingly desirable that all parts of this great Confederacy shall be at peace, and in harmony, one with another. Let us Republicans do our part to have it so. Even though much provoked, let us do nothing through passion and ill temper. Even though the southern people will not so much as listen to us, let us calmly consider their demands and yield to them if, in our deliberate view of our duty, we possibly can.*" (III, 547).

But the question remained: would the Southerners accept the reassurances of the Republicans that their institution would remain untouched in spite of Republican conviction that it was wrong? Lincoln saw that the only reassurance the South would accept was to "... cease to call slavery *wrong,* and join them in calling it *right*..." (III, 547); and this stance the Republicans could not take.

With these remarks, Lincoln's examination of the impasse between North and South was completed. In the speech he was a prosecuter; he had marshaled the evidence, had sought without success for that which would support the opposition's position, and then had drawn his conclusion. The result, implied but carefully not stated, was that the conflict was irrepressible, that the controversy had gone beyond reason or compromise, and that the "House Divided" could not long endure. There could be no middle ground, no compromise between right and wrong, he concluded; the Republicans had to and would stand fast.

With the facts before his audience, the conclusions stated, and the implications made clear, there was one thing more to be said. And in saying it Lincoln moved from the immediate to the universal, from the trial lawyer who had made a guilty verdict inevitable, to the exhorter, the poet, who appealed for the faith, the strength, and the will to go on: "Neither let us be slandered from our duty by false accusations against us, nor frightened from it by menaces of destruction to the Government nor of dungeons to ourselves. *Let us have faith that right makes might, and in that faith, let us, to the end, dare to do our duty as we understand it"* (III, 547).

Lincoln's last major speech before the Republican convention of 1860, the Cooper Union Address is at the same time the single major speech of his political career—the speech toward which thirty years of political and rhetorical apprenticeship had been pointing. In it he not only employed the techniques of the courtroom and the stump, but he carefully controlled the latter, using homely illustrations sparingly for effect, so that his logic would remain clear, his evidence unclouded, and his judgments sure. And he pointed out that the conflict was no mere poltical battle, that Douglas was no longer the symbol or focal point of the opposition, that the quarrel had indeed transcended immediacy to become truly sectional, and he saw that it could no longer be wished away by legislation or denationalization. Douglas and Lincoln, the debaters and friends, no longer exist at the end; the struggle is between competing ideologies greater than either.

But the natures of those ideologies, as Lincoln presented them, were neither complex nor legalistic; they were simple and moral. In his direct manner he defined the nature of the conflict in terms that he maintained to the end in spite of his insistence that the war was to preserve the Union. It was not a conflict between state and federal authority, nor was it a quarrel between an industrial and an agricultural economy; it was between good and evil, a conflict that, in political terms, was between the forces who supported democracy and those who denied it; and ultimately, he knew, only through permanency and supremacy of the Union could democracy win.

III   *The Decision of 1860*

Although Lincoln spoke throughout New England, his points were repetitious; his major effort had been made. In returning to Springfield, he plunged immediately into practical politics, knowing that he had at least a chance for the nomination. In April, he wrote to Lyman Trumbull, in response to a question, that "The taste *is* in my mouth a little" (IV, 45); and in May, at the convention in Decatur, he became the Illinois candidate, the rail splitter from the prairie. From Illinois he could count on twenty-two votes of the two hundred and thirty-three that were needed for the nomination. But Illinois was a critical state; in the election it could easily go to Douglas unless the Republican candidate was very strong; and, of practical political importance, the convention was to be held in Chicago.

The delegates gathered in the wooden Wigwam from Wednesday, May 16, to Friday, May 18. The array of candidates was impressive, all of them leaders of the Republican cause, representatives of powerful states, and known for their views: William H. Seward of New York, former governor, a two-term senator, and an outspoken anti-slavery man; Salmon P. Chase of Ohio, former governor and senator, more outspokenly anti-slavery than Seward; Edward Bates of Missouri; Simon Cameron of Pennsylvania; and Justice John McLean of the United States Supreme Court. Each of them was prominent in comparison to Lincoln, but each had liabilities: Seward and Chase were known as radicals; Bates had been tainted by Know-Nothingism; Cameron had a reputation for dishonesty; and McLean was too old.

Lincoln, the unknown quality, sought to be second choice of those delegates who could not abide any of the others; his campaign managers, led by David Davis, conspired to fill the Wigwam with Lincoln supporters; and four of the candidates were, against Lincoln's instructions, tempted with promises of Cabinet posts. In all, it was the American political system in operation.

The first ballot thinned the field, with Seward leading at 173½; Lincoln, surprisingly second with 102; and Cameron, Chase, and Bates, more than fifty votes behind. The second gave Seward 184½ and Lincoln 181, with the others trailing. On the third Lincoln went to 231½; the chairman of the Ohio delegation switched four votes to Lincoln; and the relatively unknown man from Illinois had become the party's candidate.

[148]

Lincoln's response to the event was formal but deeply felt. To the committee delegated to inform him that he had won, he replied:

> Deeply and even painfully sensible of the great responsibility which is inseparable from that honor—a responsibility which I could almost wish had fallen upon some one of the far more eminent men and experienced statesmen whose names were before the Convention, I shall, by your leave, consider more fully the resolutions of the Convention, denominated the platform, and without unseasonable delay, respond to you, Mr. Chairman, in writing—not doubting now, that the platform will be found satisfactory, and the nomination accepted. (IV, 51)

To Joshua Giddings, his reply was more profound: "May the Almighty grant that the cause of truth, justice, and humanity, shall in no wise suffer at my hands" (IV, 51). He was aware of the implications of his nomination and of the good chances for the party, and he was determined to play down the issue he had expressed so forthrightly that fall. Hence, the call to duty, to conflict, and to righteous victory was lost in the political reality of both the platform and the campaign Lincoln approved. Carefully balanced, the appeal was to conservatives and liberals, Whigs and Democrats, Easterners and Westerners, new and old Americans. The slavery plank, as Lincoln approved it, was moderate. Instead of the forthright opposition to slavery's spread written into the platform of 1856 and expected in this one, the new statement merely denied congressional or legislative right to legalize slavery in the territories. If the irrepressible conflict were to come at once, it would not do so at Lincoln's instigation. Anxiously at first and then with confidence he watched the confused Democrats, knowing that by August his good chance had become a certainty.

The strategy he had plotted since 1858 was a success. In the Charleston convention the split between Douglas and Buchanan became irreparable, and the convention reflected that split. Neither Douglas nor anyone else could be nominated, and the convention adjourned, to meet again in Baltimore six weeks later. There, with recalcitrant Southerners meeting in Richmond, Douglas was nominated. But the recalcitrants met again in Baltimore, passed a strong resolution protecting slavery, and nominated John C. Breckenridge of Kentucky. Hopelessly, a group of old-line Whigs and Know-Nothings formed a third party—the Constitutional Union party—and nominated John Bell of Tennessee; and the campaign began.

Lincoln remained in Springfield, publicly silent but watching closely, while Douglas campaigned furiously, determined to take his case to the people, particularly in the South. A futile but magnificent display of courage, his campaign was based on his belief that only his election could prevent war. But by October, with the results from Pennsylvania and Ohio in, he knew that he had lost. In a last burst of energy he became not a candidate but a Unionist as he went South, preaching the Union cause and even threatening upon occasion. But, while Lincoln sat silently in Springfield, Douglas became increasingly convinced that that cause, too, was hopeless.

On November 6, Lincoln, adorned by a stylish but scraggly new beard, grown at the instigation of a child aptly described as insufferable by Lord Charnwood, watched his election made fact. But it was as a minority president, polling less than half of the votes cast, that he would take office. His electoral victory was impressive, 173 to 72 for Breckenridge, 39 for Bell, and 12 for Douglas, whose popular vote was second only to Lincoln's. Yet the election was constitutional; and, as Lincoln spent the next four months waiting and preparing to take office, he saw the nation begin to disintegrate around him.

"... a new birth of freedom ..."

THE CONFUSED DRAMA of the last month of 1860 and the first two months of 1861 introduced a new element into the thinking and writing of Abraham Lincoln. Since he had first been stirred by the Nebraska Bill in 1854, he had seen the conflict between Republicans and Democrats, North and South, in moral terms as between good and evil and in political terms as between democracy and anti-democracy. Until 1854, he had accepted the premise that individual liberty and national democracy were synonymous; and his political writing reflected that acceptance, his own ideas seeking an expansion of both in traditional Whiggish terms.

The annexation of Texas, the Mexican War, and the annexation of Mexico's northern provinces began a process of education for Lincoln that ended with the debate over the Nebraska Bill, as it made clear to him that liberty and democracy were not synonymous. As the slavery crisis intensified and became continuous during the 1850's, both Whigs and Democrats tried to resolve it, the Whigs destroying themselves in the process, and the Democrats seeking to denationalize it. But the problem was too complex for the resolution proposed by Douglas. In his efforts he had failed to perceive that his proposed solutions, based upon the terms "democracy" and "liberty," were only pragmatic. But, more important, these solutions denied both terms as they were defined in the Declaration of Independence and by subsequent attempts to make that ideal a reality.

Lincoln's re-emergence was the result of his recognition that the solution promised by Douglas' bill was a mockery of the personal freedom due all men under the Declaration. Douglas would permit both liberty and the lack of it, democracy and its denial; and his solution threatened the advance of slavery into areas previously closed to it. Lincoln, stirred for the first time in his life as a man rather than as a political partisan, determined to stop that advance and to expose the promised solution for a fraud. He embarked on a course of political action as radical and potentially explosive as that he opposed, and the remainder of the decade saw Lincoln move from obscurity to the Presidency as he defined the issues with a clarity transcending the crisis itself.

To the conflict Lincoln brought personal ambition and a great deal of practical political and legal experience gathered during two decades of practicing. But these qualities were commonplaces balanced by negative qualities; and the most important of these was a compassionate nature so carefully controlled that it was almost nonexistent, and with it a lack of toleration of human weakness that verged on self-righteousness, a lack of regard for human feelings, and a satirical sense often ruthless.

But above his coolness Lincoln had an incisive mind, a passion for reason, and a respect for logic. And in the early years of the decade of crisis, personal failure and tragedy released some of the compassion in his nature, permitting him to distinguish between men and their ideas, and replacing cool detachment with passionate dedication. Lincoln the skeptical satirist gradually began to disappear; and Lincoln the humanist gradually emerged.

The years between 1845 and 1860 made Lincoln a great writer; but, as the decade closed, he had not yet become one; his works during these years were largely intellectual exercises, designed to lay bare the inevitable logic behind facts, to marshal them both clearly and precisely, and to use them to convince. Language to him remained a tool, and the results were statements that touched men's minds but rarely their hearts. In his determination to find the truth he did not touch man's sense of the infinite.

But at times toward the end of the decade, he began to attempt to do so, as he began himself to sense something of the infinite, far beyond the immediate conflict, inherent in his logic. The result was a touch of true poetic feeling that was almost lost in the sheer logical weight of his rhetoric. But in 1860, in the last major work of the decade, at the very end of his speech at the Cooper Union he strained toward perhaps the only truth that man can know: the search for truth itself and the expression of that search in one's own life. In that moment Lincoln began to become a great writer.

The decade of the 1860's, then, under the stress of personal and public tragedy and the conviction that there was meaning behind chaos, is the time during which Lincoln the great writer began to make his presence known. Significantly, during those years Lincoln's greatest works were the product of intense personal involvement and compassion, of moments in which he was most aware of the frailty, and the glory of human flesh and blood. The compassion, the deep sense of emotional involvement and commitment that he had suppressed so long, began to make itself felt; and the result was poetry.

But in the months between election and inauguration, the tragic crisis took shape. South Carolina seceded, followed by Mississippi, Florida, Alabama, Georgia, Louisiana, and Texas. Buchanan vacillated, while others sought ineffectually to act. In Springfield Lincoln stood firm, blocking compromise as he hoped that the good sense of the people would prevail. But the crisis intensified.

I   *The Trip to Washington*

The impact of secession, the threat of war, the acceptance of responsibility, the awareness that the immediate problem had become survival, and the sudden impact of the reality of what had for years been an abstract threat—all these factors combined, during those months of waiting, practical preparation, and of pondering, to bring to the surface Lincoln's long-hidden personal emotional commitment. The continued crisis then permitted it to find expression in words as simple and direct as any in his past writing, but they were now evocative of an awareness of time and eternity. At the time of leaving Springfield for Washington this new, personal, and universal human recognition made itself felt as the Lincolns boarded the special train that was to take them to the capital. At eight o'clock on the morning of Monday, February 11, 1861, the President-elect reached the platform, turned, removed his hat, and then spoke to the crowd who had come to see him off:

> My friends—No one, not in my situation, can appreciate my feeling of sadness at this parting. To this place, and the kindness

of these people, I owe every thing. Here I have lived a quarter of a century, and have passed from a young to an old man. Here my children have been born, and one is buried. I now leave, not knowing when, or whether ever, I may return, with a task before me greater than that which rested upon Washington. Without the assistance of that Divine Being, who ever attended him, I cannot succeed. With that assistance I cannot fail. Trusting in Him, who can go with me, and remain with you and be every where for good, let us confidently hope that all will yet be well. To his care commending you, as I hope in your prayers you will commend me, I bid you an affectionate farewell.[1]

The President-elect who left Springfield for Washington in 1861 was different from the brash young congressman of fourteen years before. As Lincoln journeyed east, stopping to speak and confer in the cities and towns of Indiana, Ohio, Pennsylvania, and New York, it was evident that he knew that his mission had no precedent, that he was to preside over the nation either in its death throes or as it underwent a new birth of freedom. In his speeches he refused to consider the former possibility, but its haunting presence was always evident.

At his first stop, at Tolono, Illinois, he set forth the thesis that was to lay at the heart of each speech on the way, none of them partisan, but all prayerful: "I am leaving you on an errand of national importance, attended as you are aware, with considerable difficulties. Let us believe, as some poet has expressed it:— Behind the cloud the sun is still shining" (IV, 191). The note of irony did not continue; it was replaced by a sense of history and of the past as continuity, as tradition, and as symbol.

This sense of the past, new to Lincoln except for that expressed in verse fragments years before, led him to a new concept, rooted in logic during the six years of controversy with Douglas, but now an intrinsic part of the symbolic, vivid evocation of the past that began to permeate his writing and his thinking. That concept, mystic and emotional rather than logical, was his awareness of the Union as an organic whole, transcending all particulars. No longer a political unit to Lincoln, it was a living thing that must be preserved. In Indianapolis, his first major stop, he gave voice to these feelings:

. . . if the union of these States, and the liberties of this people, shall be lost, it is but little to any one man of fifty-two years of age, but a great deal to the thirty millions of people who inhabit these United States, and to their posterity in all coming time. It is your business to rise up and preserve the Union and liberty, for yourselves, and not for me. . . .

I, as already intimated, am but an accidental instrument, temporary, and to serve but for a limited time, but I appeal to you again to constantly bear in mind that with you, and not with politicians, not with Presidents, not with office-seekers, but with you, is the question, "Shall the Union and shall the liberties of this country be preserved to the latest generation?" (IV, 194)

Taking hope from the crowds and the receptions, Lincoln began to express confidence that good will, good sense, and respect for the constitutional Union would prevail. He insisted again and again that he was temporarily but constitutionally President, that in four years Douglas or someone else would follow. In spite of a failing voice, he reiterated that his Presidency was not an end, but a beginning. At Buffalo he was soberly admonishing: "Stand up to your sober convictions of right, to your obligations to the Constitution, act in accordance with those sober convictions, and the clouds which now arise in the horizon will be dispelled, and we shall have a bright and glorious future; and when this generation has passed away, tens of thousands will inhabit this country where only thousands inhabit [it] now" (IV, 221).

As he reached New York and turned south, the reality began to become increasingly evident. In New York he stated that "There is nothing that can ever bring me willingly to consent to the destruction of this Union . . ."; and against the historic background of revolutionary strife and bloodshed in New Jersey and Pennsylvania he began to speak of fratricidal war, promising to attempt to avoid it, but not avoiding his responsibilities. To the Pennsylvania General Assembly, he made this clear:

. . . . It is not with any pleasure that I contemplate the possibility that a necessity may arise in this country for the use of the military arm. While I am exceedingly gratified to see the manifestation upon your streets of your military force here, and exceedingly gratified at your promise here to use that force upon a proper emergency, while I make acknowledgements, I desire to repeat, in order to preclude any possible misconstruction, that I do most sincerely hope that we shall have no use for them—that it will never become their duty to shed blood, and most especially never to shed fraternal blood. I promise that, (in so far as I may have wisdom to direct,) if so painful a result shall in any wise be brought about, it shall be through no fault of mine. (IV, 245)

But, as he left Harrisburg to go through Baltimore to Washington, the danger became immediate. The apparent threat to his life in Baltimore and the sadness of his passage to Washington in disguise made clear the reality and the seriousness of the crisis. Washington, an uneasy oasis in the midst of secession, began to resemble an armed camp under siege; the hope, the nostalgic appeals to the past, and the pleas for loyalty and calm began to fade away. Lincoln the pragmatic realist once more took command; but, as he waited in Willard's Hotel, he planned one more statement of principle and plea for good sense and good will.

II   *The First Inaugural Address*

When Lincoln appeared on the inaugural platform on March 4, the unfinished capitol dome looming symbolically behind him, it appeared that secession had run its course, that the remaining states were loyal, and that the dissident deep South states might yet return to their old allegiance; these, at least, were the assumptions under which Lincoln composed the final draft of his inaugural address. Turning immediately to the crisis, he attempted to reassure the South, asserting that no secession had taken place and that none would be acknowledged, as he restated the constiutional position on slavery and his own policy toward the institution in the slave states. To prove his sincerity, he emphasized the constitutionality of returning fugitive slaves and his own intention to abide by that and all provisions of the Constitution.

But these reassurances were prefatory to his statement on secession itself, and he made his position clear:

> I hold that in contemplation of universal law, and of the Constitution, the Union of these States is perpetual. Perpetuity is implied, if not expressed, in the fundamental law of all national governments. It is safe to assert that no government proper, ever had a provision in its organic law for its own termination. Continue to execute all the express provisions of our national Consti-

tution, and the Union will endure forever—it being impossible to destroy it, except by some action not provided for in the instrument itself. (IV, 264–65)

Given then the permanence of the Union and his own oath of office to support the Constitution, Lincoln found his course clear:

I therefore consider that, in view of the Constitution and the laws, the Union is unbroken; and, to the extent of my ability, I shall take care, as the Constitution itself expressly enjoins upon me, that the laws of the Union be faithfully executed in all the States. Doing this I deem to be only a simple duty on my part; and I shall perform it, so far as practicable, unless my rightful masters, the American people, shall withold the requisite means, or, in some authoritative manner, direct the contrary. I trust this will not be regarded as a menace, but only as the declared purpose of the Union that it *will* constitutionally defend, and maintain itself. (IV, 265–66)

With determination modified by consideration for local, state, and regional feelings, he turned to his declaration of immediate action in response to the alleged acts of secession. In the first draft he had stated his intention to *reclaim* governmental property already taken over, but because of the connotations of the word he carefully defined both the course and the intent of his planned actions. But the ultimate intent remained the same:

In doing this there needs to be no bloodshed or violence; and there shall be none, unless it be forced upon the national authority. The power confided to me, will be used to hold, occupy, and possess the property, and places belonging to the government, and to collect the duties and imposts; but beyond what may be necessary for these objects, there will be no invasion—no use of force against, or among the people anywhere... there will be no attempt to force obnoxious strangers among the people for that object. (IV, 266)

The principles underlying federal right and responsibility were to Lincoln clear; and he redefined them, asserting, however, that in the interest of peace, tranquillity, and understanding, he would withhold force; he would rely on reason, on mutual affection, and on national loyalty to bring the sections together.

Moderation and reconciliation dominate the rest of the speech: physically, he asserted, the states could not separate, just as politically they could not under the Constitution. There were, however, means under the Constitution by which redress might be secured, even to amending the Constitution itself; but ". . . the central idea of secession, is the essence of anarchy . . ." (IV, 268). Ultimately, therefore, the only recourse must be faith in the wisdom and justice, under God, of ". . . this great tribunal, the American people" (IV, 270).

His final words held both peace and a sword. The next to last paragraph, with which Lincoln ended the first draft, expresses definance and determination; the last expresses hope and faith. The former, in keeping with the tone of the major portion of the speech and drawing its rationale from his factual analysis of the President's duty under the Constitution, is blunt and clear in its warning: "In *your* hands, my dissatisfied fellow countrymen, and not in *mine,* is the momentous issue of civil war. The government will not assail *you.* You can have no conflict, without being yourselves the agressors. *You* have no oath registered in Heaven to destroy the government, while *I* have the most solemn one to 'preserve, protect, and defend it' " (IV, 271).

In the last paragraph, however, Lincoln again transcended the immediacy of conflict, threats, and crisis to find a mystic unity reflecting that of the physical Union and providing the spiritual bonds that hold that political relationship together in perpetuity. When he permitted his emotional faith and empathy to find expression, Lincoln's final words sought to find a meaning both spiritual and humanistic beyond the harshness of fact:

> I am loth to close. We are not enemies, but friends. We must not be enemies. Though passion may have strained, it must not break our bonds of affection. The mystic chords of memory, stretching from every battle-field, and patriot grave, to every living heart and hearthstone, all over this broad land, will yet swell the chorus of the Union, when again touched, as surely they will be, by the better angels of our nature. (IV, 271)

After a speech primarily logical and restrained, balanced by determination and a search for reconciliation, the last paragraph strives for an expression that is almost pure prose poetry in rhythm and tone. Instead of the matter-of-factness alternated by reassurances, statements of intent, and veiled defiances and dares, all of them in effect if not in intent emphasizing the fact of secession while denying it, Lincoln asserted in this final paragraph an underlying unity that no political action could deny. Here, in substance, is the mystic nature of the Union Lincoln revered.

The history of that final paragraph is curious. Lincoln had intended to end with the paragraph preceding, on a note of determination, firmness, and righteousness; but Seward, suggesting a final note of friendship and conciliation, handed Lincoln a paragraph of his own. Using Seward's paragraph and his idea as a basis, Lincoln turned the passage into poetry. Rhythm and sound, the products of a keen feeling for words, appear in the revision; abstractions become concrete, and the strong forward movement of active verbs replaces the passive stillness of Seward's suggestion. The only example surviving of Lincoln's deliberate search for a poetic effect, it was a lesson Lincoln was to apply with increasing frequency in moments of intimate personal rather than documentary public expression.

III   Realism and Idealism, 1861–1862

With the fall of Fort Sumter, the call for volunteers, the first Battle of Bull Run, the massive buildup of federal power, and the inauguration of a blockade, Lincoln the realist, basing constant decisions upon the accumulation and rational analysis of fact, once more dominated the emotionally sensitive man who had briefly emerged. The war, he knew, had to be prosecuted vigorously for the Union to be preserved; and doing so left no room for sentiment. As a writer during the war years he functioned as a rational machine, practical, pragmatic, political when necessary; he was determined that each thought, action, or spoken or written word would contribute to the successful conclusion of the war. Military, political, and diplomatic necessity became the means of the nation's continued existence, and to these Lincoln gave all his attention.

Nevertheless, in the midst of determined concentration, in moments of intense personal involvement, on both public and private occasions, the depths of his emotional awareness of the human price of Union broke through his containment. When his friend the young Colonel Elmer Ellsworth was killed at Alexandria, his body lay in state in the White House, while Lincoln wrote to his parents:

In the untimely loss of your noble son, our affliction here, is scarcely less than your own. So much of promised usefulness to one's country and of bright hopes for one's self and friends, have rarely been so suddenly dashed, as in his fall. In size, in years, and in youthful appearance, a boy only, his power to command men, was surpassingly great. This power, combined with a fine intellect, an indomitable energy, and a taste altogether military, constituted in him, as seemed to me, the best natural talent, in that department, I ever knew. And yet he was singularly modest and deferential in social intercourse. My acquaintance with him began less than two years ago; yet through the latter half of the intervening period, it was as intimate as the disparity of our ages, and my engrossing engagements, would permit. To me, he appeared to have no indulgences or pastimes; and I never heard him utter a profane, or an intemperate word. What was conclusive of his good heart, he never forgot his parents. The honors he labored for so laudably, and in the sad end, so gallantly gave his life, he meant for them, no less than for himself.

In the hope that it may be no intrusion upon the sacredness of your sorrow, I have ventured to address you this tribute to the memory of my young friend, and your brave and early fallen child.

May God give you that consolation which is beyond all earthly power. Sincerely your friend in a common affliction— (IV, 385–86)

For sensitivity, for insight into character, into the nature of grief, and for instinctively finding the right words at a time when words are inadequate, this letter, the only personal letter Lincoln had written in weeks, was almost without precedent in the Lincoln papers. Yet it does not transcend or attempt to transcend that grief in terms of a higher duty or a greater good or even the will of God. Instinctively, he knew that expressing such sentiments would be fraudulent. But at the same time the letter does not reach the level of brief, pointed poetic statement that he was to attain later. Ellsworth's death, early in the war, had not yet become part of a greater tragic and poetic whole.

Yet a few months later, in a message to Congress in Special Session on July 4, 1861, Lincoln began to reach toward that identity with the universal predicament of man. In the midst of a message examining causes, citing events, and justifying actions often horrible in their potential or their actuality, he attempted to convey something of what he saw beyond:

And this issue embraces more than the fate of these United States. It presents to the whole family of man, the question, whether a constitutional republic, or a democracy—a government of the people, by the same people—can, or cannot, maintain its territorial integrity, against its own domestic foes. It presents the question, whether discontented individuals, too few in numbers to control administration, according to organic law, in any case, can always, upon the pretences made in this case, or on any other pretences, or arbitrarily, without any pretence, break up their Government, and thus practically put an end to free government upon the earth. It forces us to ask: "Is there, in all republics, this inherent, and fatal weakness?" "Must a government, of necessity, be too *strong* for the liberties of its own people, or too *weak* to maintain its own existence?" (IV, 426)

In these questions, in Lincoln's logical approach to a problem growing out of immediate human experience and approaching the ultimate human dilemma, is suggested the answer in rededication that Lincoln was to find in three bloody days at Gettysburg two years later. But in 1861 only the conviction and the search for justification could provide a tentative answer; the final answer, he knew, could be found only in the war itself. It was a question that could be answered at the time only by a recurring assurance in the rest of the message, interspersed among facts, legal examinations, and pointed notations of the denial of equality inherent in the Secessionists' statements. In adding to that reassurance he turned again to the meaning of the Union and the war he was waging to save it:

This is essentially a People's contest. On the side of the Union, it is a struggle for maintaining in the world, that form, and substance, of government, whose leading object is, to elevate the condition of men—to lift artificial weights from all shoulders—to clear the paths of laudable pursuit for all—to afford all, an unfettered start, and a fair chance, in the race of life. Yielding to partial, and temporary departures, from necessity, this is the leading objective of the government whose existence we contend. (IV, 438)

But, while he sought to communicate that higher meaning of the war, he began to teach himself the art of war in much the same manner as he had learned grammar and mathematics years before. After the defeat at Bull Run in July, 1861, knowing that the war would not be short, he began formulating policy for the long war. Having recognized its nature before most of his contemporaries, he began to understand the nature of modern war— closing with the enemy and destroying him, while strategically cutting off supplies and destroying his will to fight at home. But it was to be years before he found a general who agreed.

During these fearful months of the summer of 1861, he began to see a spiritual signficance in the war as his fundamentalist faith, long in abeyance, suggested a meaning to the war. As he proclaimed a national fast day in August, 1861, he saw the moral implications of the war. Slavery and the attempted destruction of free institutions were evil; such actions invited, even demanded punishment by a just, personal God who knew and weighed the acts of men. The war then became both a punishment and a purging, perhaps prefatory to another resurgence of greatness under God if man were able and willing to accept and build upon the righteous punishment of God. But whether or not rebirth was to come about, the will of God in the war was clear:

> ... when our own beloved Country, once, by the blessing of God, united, prosperous and happy, is now afflicted with faction and civil war, it is peculiarly fit for us to recognize the hand of God in this terrible visitation, and in sorrowful remembrance of our own faults and crimes as a nation and as individuals, to humble ourselves before Him, and to pray for His mercy,—to pray that we may be spared further punishment, though most justly deserved; that our arms may be blessed and made effectual for the re-establishment of law, order and peace, throughout the wide extent of our country; and that the inestimable boon of civil and religious liberty, earned under His guidance and blessing, by the labors and sufferings of our fathers, may be restored in all its original excellence.—(IV, 482)

The war as national tragedy, brought about by a tragic flaw in the national morality, remained at the heart of Lincoln's view of the ultimate meaning of the conflict even to the time, almost four years later, when he looked back at a war almost won and attempted to assess its meaning. In keeping with the demands he imposed upon himself, he demanded the same acceptance of responsibility by the citizens if that flaw were to be redeemed, the evil purged, and the tragedy overcome. A time of testing and punishing by fire, the war had meaning only if the people were willing to give it that meaning, demanded by God, through going on in determination.

That Lincoln, in seeking the meaning of the war, returned to the fundamentalist awareness of the hand of God in man's affairs was no accident. The Deistic, fatalistic concept of human life in his youth, the explanation of such things in terms of chance, was defeatist as well as mocking; it denied the concepts of good and evil and the values inherent in democracy and equality by making them meaningless. In searching for the will by which man could go on in spite of horror, he found its origins in the faith that led Thomas Lincoln and thousands like him to cross the mountains in the face of an unknown no less frightening than the war. Thomas Lincoln and his contemporaries crossed the mountains in confidence that beyond it there was meaning, and his son approached the war the same way.

It was also, perhaps, the only faith that could give Lincoln the determination to go on, to seek answers to particular, individual problems in human terms even while directing a war that denied the human values he professed. The result was an increasing compassion for the individual human being that emphasized tolerance and even actions not in accord with his overwhelming objective. Thus, in abstract terms the writ of *habeas corpus* might be suspended and the dead piled up on the battlefield; but, in terms of human reality, justice still remained an attainable goal. When, for example, he was pondering the removal of General Fremont from his command in Missouri, Lincoln sought to fuse the common good and individual justice. In seeking the facts behind both, he wrote to General Samuel R. Curtis:

> Without prejudice, and looking to nothing but justice, and the public interest, I am greatly perplexed about Gen: Fremont: In your position, you can not but have a correct judgement in the case; and I beseech you to answer Gen. Cameron, when he hands you this, "Ought Gen: Fremont to be relieved from, or retained in his present command?" It shall be entirely confidential; but you can perceive how indispensable it is to justice & the public service, that I should have, an intelligent unprejudiced, and judicious opinion from some professional Military man on the spot, to assist me in the case.[2]

[163]

Sometimes, however, justice could be tempered with humanity and simple kindness; and, when such cases came to his attention, those of the little people caught up in the war, he did not hesitate to act. Nevertheless, he tried not to imply an interference with the internal functioning of a military unit. In one such case, that of one of the obscure men in the army, he wrote, in response to the most personal, publicly trivial of requests: "The bearer of this, Hugh Roden, says he is a drummer in the seventh regiment New Jersey volunteers, and wishes to be transferred to the second regiment New Jersey volunteers, to be with his brother, who is in the latter regiment. If it will not injuriously affect the service, I shall be glad for him to be obliged" (IV, 552).

This curious strain of public determination, regardless of cost in human lives, and personal, sympathetic concern for human values continued through the war, affecting his relationships with his generals, his army, his supporters, and the public; and the result was often detrimental to his own reputation and support. This result was particularly true in his attitude toward slavery, the evil that had brought about the conflict and that had to be eradicated if the country were to purge itself, and which was vitally important in affecting its ultimate outcome. Hating the institution, Lincoln nevertheless countermanded emancipation orders issued by his generals in the field, particularly Fremont in Missouri, because the national interest demanded that slavery be tolerated.

As early as November, 1861, he began to draw up plans for compensated emancipation, recognizing that only through such means could slavery be ended. In spite of its evil, it was constitutional, and in his oath he had sworn to uphold all of the Constitution, not merely selected parts, and there was no way other than constitutional means to eliminate it. The war, he asserted, was not a war to destroy slavery, but to preserve the Union, and that meant the Union as it was rather than as he hoped that it would be in the future. Abolishing slavery would make permanent the breach between North and South, drive the border states out of the Union, and make impossible a reunited, free, democratic nation finding its inspiration in literal acceptance of the faith of the eighteenth century.

This risk he could not run, as he made clear on numerous occasions, particularly in a letter to Horace Greeley, who had

been most outspoken in condemning what he regarded as vacilla-
tion. Even while planning a proclamation of emancipation as a
military measure directed at slavery only in areas under rebel
control, Lincoln kept his plans secret; but he made no secret of
his intent. Instead, he distinguished carefully between public
good and private wish:

> I would save the Union. I would save it in the shortest way
> under the Constitution. The sooner the national authority can be
> restored; the nearer the Union will be "the Union as it was." If
> there be those who would not save the Union, unless they could
> at the same time *save* slavery, I do not agree with them. If there
> be those who would not save the Union unless they could at the
> same time *destroy* slavery, I do not agree with them. My para-
> mount objective in this struggle *is* to save the Union, and it is
> *not* either to save or to destroy slavery. If I could save the Union
> without freeing any slave I would do it, and if I could save it by
> freeing *all* the slaves I would do it; and if I could save it by
> freeing some and leaving others alone I would also do that. What
> I do about slavery, and the colored race, I do because I believe
> it helps to save the Union; and what I forbear, I forbear because
> I do *not* believe it would help to save the Union. I shall do *less*
> whenever I shall believe what I am doing hurts the cause, and I
> shall do *more* whenever I shall believe doing more will help the
> cause. I shall try to correct errors when shown to be errors; and
> I shall adopt new views so fast as they shall appear to be true
> views.
>   I have here stated my purpose according to my view of *official*
> duty; and I intend no modification of my oft-expressed *personal*
> wish that all men every where could be free. (V, 388–89)

Clear, concise, lucid in its intent and execution, this letter con-
veys the dichotomy between public duty and personal desire;
and the issue of slavery, like the war itself, he saw as a public
matter to be resolved in the public interest rather than through
private whim or moral conviction. It was equally clear to him
that Union, freedom, and democracy must be synonymous; without the first, the others were impossible.

IV *The Emancipation Proclamation*

Nevertheless, just a month before, on July 22, 1862, he had
already read the first draft of the Emancipation Proclamation to

his Cabinet. This document, that was to make the war at once for the Union and against slavery, dealt with a matter Lincoln saw as clearly unconstitutional and yet, after the defeats on the Virginia Peninsula, the only course of action left to him. Consequently, he saw it as a military measure designed to strike at the rebel capacity to maintain the war, issued under his authority as commander-in-chief, rather than as a civil measure issued by a Presidential tyrant willing to ignore the constitutional rights of the people.

Nevertheless, the measure was delayed. Not only was it open to misinterpretation as the last feeble effort of a defeated government, but its effect on the border states at that time might have been disastrous; and Lincoln put it aside, to issue it after a major Union victory. The opportunity came that fall after the Battle of Antietam, the true turning point of the war; and the proclamation accomplished by military fiat what could not have been done otherwise. A measure, as Lincoln insisted, that was designed to assist in saving the Union, its effects went far beyond the course of the war. Ineffective and unenforceable in the areas in rebellion, whose slaves it ostensibly freed, it neverthless made impossible a return to the Union and Constitution as they were, as Lincoln knew well; and it was a major step toward universal emancipation by constitutional amendment, a course that would inevitably follow.

The document, as it was made public on September 22, 1862, to become effective on January 1, 1863, by Presidential proclamation, has little literary value. Unlike the Declaration of Independence, the document from which it takes its inspiration, it is not redeemed by poetic statements of man's highest ideals. It was a quasi-legal document in form and statement, and no more. This, perhaps, was carefully intended by Lincoln, so that its nature and its immediate effects could not be challenged. But in spite of its legalistic form and style as an instrument of war, it remains with the Declaration of Independence as one of the great documents of American and human history, pragmatic and at the same time idealistic, as, like its predecessor, it marked a milestone from which there could be no turning back.

V *Toward Gettysburg*

In 1862 and much of 1863, Lincoln's writing, both public and private, was compounded of strategy, logic, sympathy, exasperation, and humor as he ran the gamut of human emotions engendered by the war. In the cause of strategy, increasingly he concerned himself with the unfortunate course of events that plagued the Army of the Potomac. At the same time, he had to raise troops through the governors; and he had to allot the armed forces to meet real and imaginary dangers at the same time that, with the greatest reluctance, he had to teach McClellan and others the nature of modern war as he had learned it. After Antietam he found it necessary to lecture McClellan:

> You remember my speaking to you of what I called your over-cautiousness. Are you not over-cautious when you assume that you can not do what the enemy is constantly doing? Should you not claim to be at least his equal in prowess, and act upon the claim? . . .
> Again, one of the standard maxims of war, as you know, is "to operate upon the enemy's communications as much as possible without exposing your own." You seem to act as if this applies *against* you, but can not apply in your *favor*. Change positions with the enemy, and think you not he would break your communication with Richmond within the next twenty-four hours? (V, 460)

But so exasperating did Lincoln find what he had come to call McClellan's case of the "slows" that he revealed frustration in moments of laxity—a course that he knew was unwise in dealing with that temperamental general. Nevertheless, on one occasion, after McClellan's plea for time and support annoyed him, he expressed his exasperation: "I have just read your despatch about sore-tongued and fatiegued horses. Will you pardon me for asking what the horses of your army have done since the battle of Antietam that fatigue any thing?" (V, 474).

Occasionally, also, in lax moments Lincoln the humorist, who had learned his art on the stumps, the judicial circuits, and the gathering places of rural Illinois, made his appearance. However, his wartime humor was almost always in private, in intimate gatherings and alone, when he found release in practical, sometimes broad humor. One of the rare occasions on which he permitted himself to provoke laughter publicly was a Union meeting, serious in intent but marked by a light, almost lighthearted touch, in the dark days of August, 1862, before the Battle of

Anteitam. The meeting was brief, Lincoln made his point, and escaped in good humor:

> I believe there is no precedent for my appearing before you on this occasion, but it is also true that there is no precedent for your being here yourselves, and I offer, in justification of myself and of you, that, upon examination, I find nothing in the Constitution against. I, however, have an impression that there are younger gentlemen who will entertain you better, and better address your understanding than I will or could. . . . (V, 358)

After this introduction, punctuated by a great deal of laughter, cheers, and shouted comments, Lincoln asserted, that "I am very little inclined on any occasion to say anything unless I hope to produce some good by it" (V, 358). In that hope, he proceeded to deal, in the same light vein, with a very serious rumor—that of a major break between McClellan and the Secretary of War: "Gen. McClellan's attitude is such that, in the very selfishness of his nature, he cannot but wish to be successful, and I hope he will—and the Secretary of War is in precisely the same situation . . ." (V, 359). The reputed quarrel, he stated, had no basis in fact; McClellan was right in requesting support, the Secretary of War had none to give, and blame, if any, for the rumored break must ultimately rest with the President.

But such humor, when compared to his performances of the past, particularly to his attack on Cass in the House of Representatives almost fifteen years before, was weak indeed. When any humor appeared in the documents of the war years, it was brief, purposeful, and fleeting; he could warn against the *Monitor* "skylarking" up to Norfolk (V, 154), but his choice of words warned against lightly considered actions that appeared to be ill-advised and potentially disastrous. Humor, whether broad and bawdy or sharply satirical, was part of Lincoln's life; and it could not be eliminated easily. But during the war, with the exception of well-publicized instances, there are remarkably few verified examples of Lincoln's humor in action.

Significantly, one document, apparently written for his own eyes and use, dating from the fall of 1862, gives clear indication that, in moments of intense emotional concern, Lincoln turned away from humor to religious introspection in his concern for identifying the nature and purpose of the war. This doc-

ument—a brief, prayer-like essay or meditation on the will of God
as it was manifested in the war—indicates a personal concern far
deeper and more uncertain than that which he displayed or cited
in public. Simple, profound in its uncertainty, and marked by
the attempt to analyze logically what cannot be, it ends in the
wonder typical of the seeker who attempts, without dogmatism
or sectarianism, to probe and understand the Divine mind as it
is manifested in human affairs:

> The will of God prevails. In great contests each party claims
> to act in accordance with the will of God. Both *may* be, and one
> *must* be wrong. God can not be *for*, and *against* the same thing
> at the same time. In the present civil war it is quite possible that
> God's purpose is something different from the purpose of either
> party—and yet the same instrumentalities, working just as they
> do, are of the best adaption to effect His purpose. I am almost
> ready to say this is probably true—that God wills this contest,
> and wills that it shall not end yet. By his mere quiet power, on
> the minds of the now contestants, He could have either *saved*
> or *destroyed* the Union without a human contest. Yet the contest
> began. And having begun He could give the final victory to
> either side any day. Yet the contest proceeds. (V, 403–4)

Never certain of the will of God in spite of his lasting certainty that it was manifested in the war, Lincoln continued to
assert that the ultimate meaning of the war far outweighed the
fact of the struggle itself. He was convinced that it was momentous in human history; at the same time, in the national sense,
it was, however bloody, a temporary phenomenon, just as the
separation was, by all rules of logic and morality, itself temporary. As he closed the year of 1862, in his annual message to
Congress he included these ponderings:

> Our national strife springs not from our permanent part, not
> from the land we inhabit; not from our national homestead.
> There is no possible severing of this, but would multiply, and
> not mitigate, evils among us. In all its adaptations and aptitudes,
> it demands union and abhors separation. In fact, it would, ere
> long, force re-union, however much of blood and treasure the
> separation might have cost.

> Our strife pertains to ourselves—to the passing generations of
> men; and it can, without convulsion, be hushed forever with the
> passing of one generation. (V, 529)

Yet the fact itself would, he asserted, have tremendous and far-reaching effects on future generations who would ponder and ultimately evaluate the actions of those now living:

> Fellow-citizens, *we* cannot escape history. We of this Congress and this administration, will be remembered in spite of ourselves. No personal significance, or insignificance, can spare one or another of us. The fiery trial through which we pass, will light us down, in honor or dishoner, to the latest generation. We *say* we are for the Union. The world will not forget that we say this. We know how to save the Union. The world knows we do know how to save it. We—even *we here*—hold the power, and bear the responsibility. In giving freedom to the *slave,* we *assure* freedom to the *free*—honorable alike in what we give, and what we preserve. We shall nobly save, or meanly lose, the last best, hope of earth. Other means may succeed; this could not fail. The way is plain, peaceful, generous, just—a way which, if followed, the world will forever applaud, and God must forever bless. (V, 537)

As the year turned into 1863, the most momentous and dramatic year of the war, and as the great Northern generals came to the fore with spectacular victories and the casualty lists grew longer, Lincoln's awareness of the meaning of the war and the greatness of its price became certainty. In the West, Grant moved relentlessly toward Vicksburg; and, in the East, the Army of the Potomac faltered toward its trial and triumph at Gettysburg. And Lincoln, no longer pondering, waited and watched reports from the telegraph office, as he prayed that the national will might be strong enough to do what had to be done. The war had transcended its immediate cause and purpose; it had become a war for human freedom. And Lincoln learned, as had Jefferson almost a century before, that the price of freedom is extremely high.

In the early months of 1863, while waiting, maneuvering, serving, wondering, filling his moments with the diverse details of administration, strained at home, as he had been since the death of his son Willie in February of the previous year, one death among many, and yet one death, Lincoln made his final insight into the ultimate good beyond horror. In those months he became capable of making clear that reality that he knew existed somewhere in time and eternity. Consequently, with the confidence born of knowledge, while yet determined to find the public and military will to win, he made, for a time, General Hooker his instrument, demanding that he "Beware of rashness, but with energy and sleepless vigilance, go forward, and give us victories" (VI, 79).

CHAPTER 9

"The Almighty has His own purposes"

WITH ANTIETAM and the Emancipation Proclamation behind him, Lincoln was convinced that the war might be brought to a successful conclusion in 1863, that the will of God had revealed itself, and that emancipation was not far off. But Grant seemed to dally before Vicksburg, and a general had not yet been found for the East. Nevertheless, Lincoln felt that the war had become its own justification, and that a final, massive battle would see it through.

As Vicksburg fell and Gettysburg was won without a final climactic confrontation, it appeared to Lincoln that he might have been mistaken, that, although he had met and overcome his own personal crisis in the war, the nation had not yet done so. Draft riots in New York and elsewhere, a war weariness marked by a sudden surge of desertions and a climbing execution rate with which he attempted to cope in his usual attempt to strike a balance between the public good and private mercy, and countless personal attacks, both because he had issued the Emanicaption Proclamation and because it was not universal, all took their toll in that indecisive year. The cause had been defined, the course set, and the power arrayed; but the war went relentlessly on.

During 1863 three major factors plagued him: public lack of understanding of his limited emancipation policy; a future course of action toward a restored South; and the lack of national understanding of the meaning of the war. Overwhelming all, dominating it all, was the war itself, the national tragedy compounded of countless personal tragedies for which he took responsibility. Each of these problems occupied his attention and found expression in his writing during that year as he found it necessary to deal with each in the midst of routine and crisis. All of them collectively were to make themselves felt in the brief, simple statement he made at Gettysburg as the year moved toward its close.

The debate surrounding the Emancipation Proclamation was perhaps the easiest with which to deal; it had been a matter of logically, constitutionally, and militarily attacking a problem at the heart of the war itself; and the admittedly limited and temporary solution, as Lincoln saw it, could only be found in those terms rather than on a personal or moral basis. But explanations and justifications were undesirable on a public basis; the fact had to stand as it was, clearly defined in the formal legal phraseology of the document itself. Yet insistence that he explain or justify went on, and on personal bases he attempted to do so, for private rather than public information. On one occasion, at the demand of General John McClernand, a powerful political general, he wrote:

> After the commencement of hostilities I struggled nearly a year and a half to get along without touching the "institution"; and when finally I conditionally determined to touch it, I gave a hundred days fair notice of my purpose.... They chose to disregard it, and I made the peremptory proclamation on what appeared to me to be a military necessity. And being made, it must stand....
>
> As to any dread of my having a "purpose to enslave, or exterminate, the whites of the South," I can scarcely believe that such dread exists. It is too absurd. I believe you can be my personal witness that no man is less to be dreaded for undue severity, in any case. (VI, 48–49)

Yet in congratulations and in pledges of support and sympathy that came in from workmen and well-wishers in Europe he saw the impossibility of recognition or of support for the Confederacy from abroad; and he received expression of the universal human instinct for freedom, even from those suffering privation from a war in which they had no personal stake. The result was reassurance for his conviction that the war was of major significance in the history of human freedom. Yet, he was afraid, the American people had not yet come to understand and accept that fact as had workmen abroad. In this spirit, with the war apparently stalemated and with cries for peace heard in the North, he issued his proclamation for a national fast day as the spring campaigns opened. Again he sought humility, acceptance, and dedication by his people:

And, insomuch as we know that, by His divine law, nations like individuals are subjected to punishments and chastisements in this world, may we not justly fear that the awful calamity of civil war, which now desolates the land, may be but a punishment, inflicted upon us, for our presumptuous sins, to the needful end of our national reformation as a whole People? We have been the recipients of the choicest bounties of Heaven. We have been preserved, these many years, in peace and prosperity. We have grown in numbers, wealth and power, as no other nation has ever grown. But we have forgotten God. We have forgotten the gracious hand which preserved us in peace, and multiplied and enriched and strengthened us; and we have vainly imagined, in the deceitfulness of our hearts, that all these blessings were produced by some superior wisdom and virtue of our own. Intoxicated with unbroken success, we have become too self-sufficient to feel the necessity of redeeming and preserving grace, too proud to pray to the God that made us.

It behooves us then, to humble ourselves before the offended power, to confess our national sins, and to pray for clemency and forgiveness. (VI, 156)

Increasingly puritanical and fundamentalist in regarding the war as punishment inflicted by the heavy hand of God operating in man's affairs, Lincoln nevertheless forced its vigorous prosecution. As the final envelopment of Vicksburg came nearer and as the Eastern armies maneuvered toward their confrontation in a small southern Pennsylvania town, his concern intensified. A frightening dream engendered a quick telegram to his wife: "Think you better put 'Tad's' pistol away. I had an ugly dream about him" (VI, 256). He examined new weapons; he called for more militia to reinforce the army for the summer campaign; and he attempted to still the perennial fears in Washington and in the North while freeing the army to fight its final campaign. Above all, the commutations and delays of execution went on, as Lincoln probed the problem of farm boys caught in relentless destruction as the armies closed.

July was climactic, but it was not decisive. Grant in the West delivered Vickburg, and, Lincoln wrote, "The Father of Waters again goes unvexed to the sea" (VI, 409); but at Gettysburg his latest general, Meade, had lacked the final resolution. Although the North was saved and Lee's army was punished dreadfully, it had escaped to fight again. Lincoln's view of the victories was realistic; to Grant, with whom he began to feel an understanding kinship, he wrote: "I now wish to make the personal acknowledgement that you were right and I was wrong" (VI, 326). To Meade, he was bluntly honest: "... I do not believe you appreciate the magnitude of the misfortune involved in Lee's escape. He was within your easy grasp, and to have closed upon him would, in connection with our other late successes, have ended the war. As it is, the war will be prolonged indefinitely" (VI, 328).

The climactic year of 1863 had come, personal courage had never been higher; and yet, as Lincoln knew, the will that could only come from faith and dedication was lacking; and the supreme effort had yet to be made. Grant, who like Lincoln, understood the nature of war in those terms, was to come East to provide the instrument; but Lincoln determined that the national will, vital to the ultimate effort, must be supplied by the people. A proclamation of Thanksgiving, issued in July, was designed to concentrate and multiply that will through a day of national prayer that the victories might presage the end, that the people might beg God "... to subdue the anger, which has produced, and so long sustained a needless and cruel rebellion..." (VI, 332), and yet the war went on.

However, Lincoln was still convinced that the end was in sight, and problems of restoring the Union, while maintaining the national will to the end, occupied his attention. Grant's reputation for intemperance, like that of the army, was unimportant in spite of moralistic complaints that lost sight of the supreme morality in the face of minor transgressions. A temperance man by rule of logic rather than moral persuasion, Lincoln dismissed accusations of drunkenness in the army with wry acknowledgment:

> ... You have suggested that in an army—our army—drunkenness is a great evil, and one which, while it exists to a very great extent, we cannot expect to overcome so entirely as to leave [have?] such successes in our arms, as we might have without it. This undoubtedly is true, and while it is, perhaps, rather a bad source to derive comfort from, nevertheless, in a hard struggle, I do not know but what it is some consolation to be aware that there is some intemperance on the other side, too, and that they have no right to beat us in physical combat on that ground. (VI, 487)

I *The Gettysburg Address*

As 1863 drew to its close and it became evident that there would be no decision that year, Lincoln's attention, like that of the North, was drawn once more to the town of Gettysburg, where a portion of the battlefield was to become a permanent cemetery for the Union dead. In the meanwhile, however, Lincoln's confidence in the outcome of the war had been shaken by the near-disaster at Chickamauga and Chattanooga at the end of September. But the near-disaster did not become one because of the will of the Westerners, and the off-year elections gave Lincoln encouragement and support to an unexpected degree. His confidence restored, he could say again, as he had at the end of August:

> . . . Thanks to all: for the great republic—for the principle it lives by and keeps alive—for man's vast future—thanks to all.
>
> Peace does not appear so distant as it did. I hope it will come soon, and come to stay; and so come as to be worth the keeping in all future time. It will then have been proved that among free men there can be no successful appeal from the ballot to the bullet, and that they who take such appeal are sure to lose their case and pay the cost. And then there will be some black men who can remember that with silent tongue, and clenched teeth, and steady eye, and well-poised bayonet, they have helped mankind on to this great consummation, which I fear there will be some white ones unable to forget that with malignant heart and deceitful speech they strove to hinder it.
>
> Still, let us not be over-sanguine of a speedy final triumph. Let us be quite sober. Let us diligently apply the means, never doubting that a just God, in his own good time, will give us the rightful result.[1]

As the dedication of the cemetery at Gettysburg neared, these were the thoughts that dominated Lincoln's consciousness; he was confident and yet cautious, aware of the enormity of the price paid and still to be paid for freedom, and yet convinced that no price was too high if the people were determined to be free. Consequently, when Lincoln was asked to appear at the dedication, he surprised his Cabinet by consenting to go. Leaving his son Tad ill in Washington, himself worn and ill, he went by special train to Gettysburg. During the trip he worked on a brief address he had begun in Washington.

The evening of November 18, while staying at the home of Judge David Wells, he was greeted by serenaders; kindly and firmly he refused to make an address: "In my position it is somewhat important that I should not say any foolish things. . . . It very often happens that the only way to help it is to say nothing at all" (VII, 17). If he were to say anything foolish at Gettysburg —and he was concerned that he might—it would be at the ceremony the next day.

At eleven o'clock the next morning the procession, with Lincoln on horseback, moved out to the cemetery. His speech, once more revised, in his pocket, he rode where troops had deployed and fought such a short time before; and he must have been aware of the fact of the battle as well as its significance as he rode, looking out over the still-torn terrain, softened by the haze of late fall.

As the ceremony began, each speaker attempted to convey in words the nature of that struggle; the Reverend Dr. Stockton, the clergyman who gave the opening prayer, gave an exhortative oration which saw the battle as God's divine rescue; the Marine Band played "Old Hundred," and then Edward Everett, the orator of the day, rose to speak. For two hours, in the powerful style of what has been called America's "golden age of oratory," he gave one of his finest performances. Classic in form, Classical in reference, it was oratory on the grand, eloquent, orotund scale that had made him the greatest speaker of that era. He held his audience spellbound by the music of his voice, the perfection of his gestures, the appropriateness of his sentiments as he explored historical precedent, destroyed the Confederate cause, and retold the epic story of the battle. When he finished, the applause rang from the surrounding hills.

The Baltimore Glee Club followed with an appropriate dirge, composed for the occasion by Benjamin French; and then Marshall Ward Lamon, Lincoln's former law partner, announced "The President of the United States." Lincoln rose, glanced at his two-page manuscript, and nervously began:

> Four score and seven years ago our fathers brought forth on this continent, a new nation, conceived in Liberty, and dedicated to the proposition that all men are created equal.
>
> Now we are engaged in a great civil war, testing whether that nation, or any nation so conceived and so dedicated, can long

endure. We are met on a great battle-field of that war. We have come to dedicate a portion of that field, as a final resting place for those who here gave their lives that this nation might live. It is altogether fitting and proper that we should do this.

But, in a larger sense, we can not dedicate—we can not conse-crate—we can not hallow—this ground. The brave men, living and dead, who struggled here, have consecrated it, far above our poor power to add or detract. The world will little note, nor long remember what we say here, but it can never forget what they did here. It is for us the living, rather, to be dedicated here to the unfinished work which they who fought here have thus far so nobly advanced. It is rather for us to be here dedicated to the great task remaining before us—that from these honored dead we take increased devotion to that course for which they gave the last full measure of devotion—that we here highly resolve that these dead shall not have died in vain—that this nation, under God, shall have a new birth of freedom—and that government of the people, by the people, for the people, shall not perish from the earth.[2]

The speech was so short that it was over almost before it began, before the photographer could adjust his equipment, and it was a failure. As the President sat down, applause was tardy and polite; and he was convinced, as he told Lamon, that it would not "scour," that the people were disappointed. Press comments were for the most part perfunctory; the speech was criticized by Democratic papers and praised by Republicans. But it had been said as Lincoln wanted to say it, even adding the words "under God" while he spoke; and it said what he meant, what he felt, and what he knew had to be said. He returned to Washington to a sickbed with a mild case of small-pox, something, he said, which he could give everyone; and he turned his attention once more to the war, to the decisive battle then shaping up under Grant at Chattanooga in the West, and the war went on.

The brief speech, however, began to have its effect far beyond the sickroom or the hills of Gettysburg, and, in the century that followed, no other piece of brief prose has received a fraction of the attention given it. The praise, examination, analysis, and comment recognize it as one of the great American utterances; Carl Sandburg has called it "The Great American Poem." Its origins have been traced, its words counted and classified etymologically, its rhythm scanned, its form belatedly identified as classic, and its importance noted annually on May 30.

What has not been noted is its contemporaneity, its expression, as clearly as could be done, in words as appropriate as could be found, of the nature of the war's tragedy as it related to the hope and will of man. Nor has it been noted that Lincoln's few words did not make up a public statement; instead, like his earlier attempt to determine the will of God as it manifested itself in the war, it was entirely personal, and its intent was not to exhort or to cheer, but to share that personal significance with others. A tribute and a dedication, it was at the same time a prayer. The past, Lincoln hoped and believed, was prefatory to a new future, a new freedom, that gave meaning and purpose to the rows of new graves; and, as he spoke, he might have been alone. In the light of the immediate reaction perhaps he wished he had been. He had laid himself bare, and the result had, momentarily but surely, been lost in the shadow of words to all but a few.

II   *The Movement Toward Peace*

As he summed up the activities of 1863 Lincoln noted progress, and he gave much attention to the nation as a growing domestic power before noting the course of action necessary for the future if the national will and renewed dedication were to have purpose or meaning. Emancipation was proceeding, and the borders of the Confederacy were shrinking. It was necessary then to proceed with the reconstruction of the nation, and he proclaimed amnesty, easy and uncoercive to all except a few, by means of which the disaffected states could, without reprisal or harshness, take their place once more in the federal Union. As 1864 opened, Lincoln was confident but determined that freedom and equality must prevail. A letter from him found on the body of General Wadsworth, killed in the Wilderness and reprinted in the *Southern Advocate,* made that clear:

> How to better the condition of the colored race has long been a study which has attracted my serious and careful attention; hence I think I am clear and decided as to what course I shall pursue in the premises, regarding it a religious duty, as the na-

tion's guardian of these people, who have so heroically vindicated
their manhood on the battle-field, where, in assisting to save the
life of the Republic, they have demonstrated in blood their right
to the ballot, which is but the humane protection of the flag they
have so fearlessly defended.

The restoration of the Rebel States to the Union must rest
upon the principle of civil and political equality of both races;
and it must be sealed by general amnesty. (VII, 101–2)

Equality, amnesty, and compassion dominated his thinking
throughout the year 1864, which promised to be decisive; but it
ended with casualties almost beyond comprehension and with
the war still unfinished. To Secretary of War Stanton, Lincoln
pleaded for mercy for those who had become victims of war,
particularly of its bureaucracy: prisoners of war who were eager
to fight no more; discharged officers whose reputations had been
unjustly stained; the innocent families of rebels; people who
wished to join their families in the South. The commutations
went on, even for rebellious Indians; with victory in sight, Lincoln had begun to construct the foundations of peace.

But 1864 did not bring peace; instead, the summer campaign,
begun in confidence, ended in stalemate as Grant, the general
Lincoln had sought, took command in the East with the mission
of smashing Lee and ending the war. Understanding war as
Lincoln understood it, Grant had been advised of Lincoln's confidence, his support, and his hope; ". . . with a brave Army, and a
just cause," Lincoln wrote, "may God sustain you" (VII, 534) in
the course of the campaign designed to end the war.

But that conclusion was still dependent on the will of the people, and 1864, the year of the hammering campaign against Lee
and Richmond, was a Presidential election year. Peace Democrats, "copperheads," and disenchanted and Radical Republicans,
together with the personal ambitions of some upon whom Lincoln depended in their official capacities, all threatened that
necessary mandate from the people, to whom he could offer only
higher casualties, a promise, and a plea for the strength to go on.
The summer and fall of 1864 were both crucial and dangerous,
and in the course of them Lincoln almost lost faith, not in the
force of federal arms or the justice of its cause, but in the will
of the people to sustain either. To an increasing segment of the
public, horrified by the casualty lists of Grant's campaign in

Virginia, it appeared that the war was lost, that the cause was a failure.

So grim was the outlook on August 23 that Lincoln had his Cabinet sign a pledge unread, to be opened after the fall election: "This morning, as for some days past, it seems exceedingly probable that this administration will not be re-elected. Then it will be my duty to so co-operate with the President elect, as to save the Union between the election and the inauguration; as he will have secured his election on such ground that he can not possibly save it afterwards" (VII, 514).

Lincoln's opponent, General McClellan, a War Democrat, was running on a Peace Democrat platform; and he was immensely popular both with the troops he had led and with their people at home. His candidacy had gained much support from the military reverses during July and August. Grant was stalemated in Virginia, as was Sherman in Georgia; and the Confederates under General Jubal Early had once more broken into Pennsylvania. But just as the gloom seemed deepest—and many observers saw the summer of 1864 as the darkest days of the war—victories by Admiral Farragut at Mobile Bay and by Sherman at Atlanta reversed the trend, and on September 3, Lincoln proclaimed a day of Thanksgiving and prayer. Although the outcome of the election was still uncertain, the West had produced two more of its victories; and the spirits of both Lincoln and the nation were raised. A massive effort was planned to get out the soldier vote, overwhelming for Lincoln in spite of the army's fondness for its dashing and solicitous former commander, "Little Mac."

By October the trend against Lincoln's administration was reversed; the three states voting that month, Ohio, Indiana, and Pennsylvania, gave Lincoln safe majorities. In November his mandate was made clear; he had carried every state except Kentucky, Delaware, and New Jersey; and he now knew that the war would end successfully as the returns evidenced the will of the people to see it through. Extemporaneously he gave voice to his faith and his satisfaction:

> ... I am grateful to God for the approval of the people; but, while deeply grateful for this mark of their confidence in me, if I know my heart, my gratitude is free from any taint of personal triumph. I do not impugn the motives of any one opposed to me.

It is no pleasure to triumph over any one, but I give thanks to the Almighty for this evidence of the people's resolution to stand by free government and the rights of humanity. (VIII, 96)

The next evening he spoke again from a prepared text that was obviously the product of much thought. He spoke on the nature of the democratic process, even in time of crisis, in a free society, and the substance of his remarks would perhaps not have been greatly different had he lost the election:

It has long been a grave question whether any government, not *too* strong for the liberties of its people, can be strong *enough* to maintain its own existence, in great emergencies.

On this point the present rebellion brought our republic to a severe test; and a presidential election occuring in regular course during the rebellion added not a little to the strain. If the loyal people, *united,* were put to the utmost of their strength by the rebellion, must they not fail when *divided,* and partially paralyzed, by a political war among themselves?

But the election was a necessity.

We can not have free government without elections; and if the rebellion could force us to forego, or postpone a national election, it might fairly claim to have already conquered and ruined us. . . . (VIII, 100–101)

As he concluded his remarks, according to John Hay, he turned from the window. "'Not very graceful,' he said, 'but I am growing old enough not to care much for the manner of doing things.'"

III   *The Letter to Mrs. Bixby*

Yet Lincoln did care just a few days later about the manner and the sentiment when he wrote the most famous of his letters, that to Mrs. Lydia Bixby of Massachusetts, who, he had been told, had had five sons killed in action. Although later investigation has shown that the report was in error, that fact detracts nothing from the sentiment, the sincerity, and the remarkable appropriateness with which Lincoln wrote her:

Dear Madam—I have been shown, in the files of the War Department a statement of the Adjutant General of Massachusetts, that you are the mother of five sons who have died gloriously on the field of battle.

I feel how weak and fruitless must be any words of mine which should attempt to beguile you from the grief of a loss so overwhelming. But I cannot refrain from tendering to you the consolation that may be found in the thanks of the Republic they died to save.

I pray that our Heavenly Father may assuage the anguish of your bereavement, and leave you only the cherished memory of the loved and lost, and the solemn pride that must be yours, to have laid so costly a sacrifice upon the altar of Freedom.

Yours, very sincerely and respectfully,

A. LINCOLN
(VIII, 116–17)

Like the Gettysburg Address, this letter was the product of a long-felt empathy that he had been unable to express except in such moments; it notes the price, simply, starkly, and poetically; and it recognizes and feels that price as personal tragedy to the poor mother and to himself. Again, however, Lincoln's personal grief, as clearly as it is expressed, is transcended by the cause of freedom, itself greater than life; and the "solemn pride" of that knowledge is the recognition of that supreme value. Here, too, his power of expression is a manifestation of the depth of his feeling and the certainty of his faith in the future.

IV *The Second Inaugural Address*

On December 25 he received a Christmas gift—the city of Savannah, captured by Sherman. The Confederacy had been cut in two, and Lincoln prepared his missions to restore the federal authority through the South. On February 1 he signed the Thirteenth Amendment to the Constitution, that which would end slavery in the states forever. As he stood on the inaugural platform on March 4, 1865, with the war almost over, he felt his confidence and faith justified; and once more he spoke the private sentiments that he could so rarely express in public. First he looked at the occasion in its relationship to the previous inaugural and to the immediate present:

At this second appearing to take the oath of the presidential office, there is less occasion for an extended address than there was at first. Then a statement, somewhat in detail, of a course to be pursued, seemed fitting and proper. Now, at the expiration of four years, during which public declarations have been constantly called forth on every point and phase of the great contest which still absorbs the attention, and engrosses the energies of the nation, little that is new could be presented. The progress of our arms, upon which all else chiefly depends, is as well known to the public as to myself; and it is, I trust, reasonably satisfactory and encouraging to all. With high hope for the future, no prediction in regard to it is ventured. (VIII, 332)

Again looking at the past, he described the beginning of the war:

On the occasion corresponding to this four years ago, all thoughts were anxiously directed to an impending civil-war. All dreaded it—all sought to avert it. While the inaugural address was being delivered from this place, devoted altogether to *saving* the Union without war, insurgent agents were in the city seeking to *destroy* it without war—seeking to dissol[v]e the Union, and divide effects, by negotiation. Both parties deprecated war; but one of them would *make* war rather than let the nation survive; and the other would *accept* war rather than let it perish. And the war came. (VIII, 332)

Behind the war was its cause, a cause Lincoln never doubted.

One eighth of the whole population were colored slaves, not distributed generally over the Union, but localized in the Southern part of it. These slaves constituted a peculiar and powerful interest. All knew that this interest was, somehow, the cause of the war. To strengthen, perpetuate, and extend this interest was the object for which the insurgents would rend the Union, even by war; while the government claimed no right to do more than to restrict the territorial enlargement of it. Neither party expected for the war, the magnitude, or the duration, which it has already attained. Neither anticipated that the *cause* of the conflict might cease with, or even before, the conflict itself should cease. Each looked for an easier triumph, and a result less fundamental and astounding. Both read the same Bible and pray to the same God; and each invokes His aid against the other. It may seem strange that any men should dare to ask a just God's assistance in wringing their bread from the sweat of other men's faces; but let us judge not that we be not judged. (VIII, 332–33)

From the cause, Lincoln looked to the meaning of the war; and in turning to it, in the sonorous tones of the English Bible, he moved, as he had at Gettysburg, into the realm of poetry:

The prayers of both could not be answered; that of neither has been answered fully. The Almighty has His own purposes. "Woe unto the world because of offences! for it must needs be that offenses come; but woe to that man by whom the offence cometh." If we shall suppose that American Slavery is one of those offences which, in the providence of God, must needs come, but which, having continued through His appointed time, He now wills to remove, and that He gives to both North and South, this terrible war, as the woe due to those by whom the offence came, shall we discern therein any departure from those divine attributes which the believers in a Living God always ascribe to Him? Fondly do we hope—fervently do we pray—that this mighty scourge of war may speedily pass away. Yet if God wills that it continue, until all the wealth piled by the bond-man's two hundred and fifty years of unrequited toil shall be sunk, and until every drop of blood drawn with the lash, shall be paid by another drawn with the sword, as was said three thousand years ago, so still it must be said "the judgements of the Lord, are true and righteous altogether." (VIII, 333)

The meaning of the war defined, it remained to translate that meaning into action, into a program fusing the real and the ideal: "With malice toward none; with charity for all; with firmness in the right, as God gives us to see the right, let us strive on to finish the work we are in; to bind up the nation's wounds; to care for him who shall have borne the battle, and for his widow, and his orphan—to do all which may achieve and cherish a just, and lasting peace, among ourselves, and with all nations" (VIII, 333).

In his final formal address Lincoln achieved the heights of noble human emotion; and the words, the phrases, the rhythms are natural reflections of it. Love and forgiveness, faith and dedication, hope and acceptance are the stuff by which man survives and prevails, in life or in death; and Lincoln, near the close of a great war and a great life, came to the realization and assertion of the only values that give it meaning. A realist, his realism went beyond the surface of life to probe its very meaning; and in this, his last attempt at definition, he made that meaning as clear as he found it, and he pointed out the way by which it might be lived.

In the last weeks, as the end of the war and of Lincoln's life came nearer, Lincoln the realist took control once more. Confideut that he had told the truth in his inaugural address, knowing that "Men are not flattered by being shown that there has been a difference of purpose between them and the Almighty" (VIII, 356), yet accepting that knowledge with humility, he counseled General Grant to "Let the *thing* be pressed" (VIII, 392); and it was. A week later, having seen it pressed, he sought relaxation. The next day he was dead.

CHAPTER 10

"Everything I say, you know, goes into print"

A T LINCOLN'S death his place in American history was secure; in the military, political, social, and intellectual history of the nation he had made marks that could only grow with the years. But his place in literary history was uncertain, although it too has grown with the years until it is as secure today as his place in the grand panorama of the American past. Yet when attempts are made to assess the nature and basis of that reputation, the assessors often take refuge in laudatory generalities or in close analysis of origins, influences, and poetic techniques. Such, unfortunately, has been the fate of the Gettysburg Address; reduced to an academic metrical exercise, it loses both meaning and being in the process.

Conventional techniques of structural analysis, it is evident, can be applied freely to a great deal of Lincoln's writing; much of his prose is rhythmic in the great tradition of the King James Bible, reflecting his keen ear for the music of words. Alliteration, assonance, imagery, and analogy, together with phrases of succinct vividness, abound in his most deeply felt works. But these characteristics do not belong uniquely to Lincoln; they are shared by many lesser writers. Nor, it is important to note, are they the essence of Lincoln's greatness; they are merely a part of a prose style that grows out of the fundamentals of human experience and reaches for the heights of human aspiration, an intensity of emotion that can be felt and expressed only rarely.

Evidence of this achievement, as rare in Lincoln's own writing as it is in American literary history, can be found in the fact that, in spite of the universal acknowledgment of his greatness, no conventional literary category can satisfactorily be applied to his works. Called an orator by those who earliest recognized his literary abilities, he was no orator; called a poet in the broad twentieth-century definition of the word, he was not a poet. And yet, at the same time, he was both of these and much more. At his best he evoked, in simple, dignified poetic prose, the essence of the American experience.

Lincoln was realist and idealist in the tradition that has characterized America from its beginning, that characterizes it today, and that hopefully will characterize it as long as the nation exists. In his life those elements of realism, an identity with and understanding of man's total physical environment, and idealism, an intellectual and emotional perception of the great humanistic potential of man, became fused in the midst of the Civil War, the national tragedy and the national crucible that brought the real and the ideal closer to a fusion in the national character than it had ever been before. Lincoln's function, his purpose as President and as writer, was to probe that experience and to define it for all time to come.

The American ideal was stated without qualification in the eighteenth century, and that statement was coincidental with the birth of the country. But words are meaningless until they take on the dimensions of life from life itself. During the years between the Declaration of Independence and the domestic crisis of the middle of the nineteenth century that ideal had taken on the dimensions of life as it began to find its roots in the American experience; and it began to expand, demanding the ultimate definition of the ideal in terms of the reality. The means by which that ultimate definition was made real was the war itself.

At the heart of this movement toward an ultimate fusion of real and ideal was the role of the individual, for whose benefit the ideal had been stated in the rational terms of the eighteenth century. The years of the first half of the nineteenth century marked, after an initial period of uncertainty, a steady movement toward expanding the role of the individual in almost every area of American society—particularly in the political, social, and economic realms. Jeffersonian democracy, which had taken as its substance the American ideal, gave way to the pragmatic, dynamic years of Jacksonian democracy and the common man— the years during which Union, liberty, and democracy became synonymous. But that definition, as expanded as it became, had also remained limited by the barriers of race and jingoism.

This was the American experience, manifested most completely in the geographic dynamism of the frontier, which Abraham Lincoln knew in his formative years; and the writings of Lincoln are the result of the impact of that experience, both in its movement toward the ideal and in its inherent denials of the ideal, upon Lincoln's natural intellect and his emotional sensitivity. The course of Lincoln's life through his fortieth year was compounded of learning to examine the strengths and the shortcomings of that experience as he knew it and saw it in the world around him. It was evident to him before he was twenty-one that, in spite of the pronouncements of Jackson and his followers, the real and the ideal were still far apart. Nevertheless, much of his adulthood was spent pursuing the reality of a society open to the white Anglo-Saxon majority. But even in those years he did not lose sight of the gulf that still remained between the ideal and the real; instead he accepted, as he was to do to the end of his life, the constitutional and social limitations upon the movement toward complete fusion of real and ideal, while his intellectual insight told him that within those limitations there was a way whereby the two might eventually become one. But he could not ignore the fact that the discrepancy remained, and his concern with it intensified as it seemed to broaden and deepen in the late 1840's and early 1850's and the constitutional restrictions remained.

During these years Lincoln had become an effective and pragmatic but not great writer. From near-illiteracy he had, through his own sharp intellect and his restless ambition, mastered the tools of language at the same time that he gained a great deal of insight into the tragicomedy of the human situation and of the ultimate hope for man in the rule of reason. Logician, humorist, satirist, realist, he remained during his maturity a pragmatic man of the eighteenth century, carefully controlled, rational, and convinced that the ultimate order of the American ideal could and would eventually become real.

But suddenly in the decade of the 1850's he became a man of the nineteenth century, a man who recognized that reason could take man only part of the way toward that ideal. From that point on, a man was on his own, able to seek the ultimate ideal only through abstractions of justice and mercy not embodied in the man's experience. This discovery led him to faith, a faith in the ultimate reality of those abstractions beyond man's environment and his experience. This discovery provided the basis for Lincoln's greatness both as a man and a writer; and, as it merged with his insight into the human predicament, it provided the substance of his greatest writings. Literary technique, the form through which they found expression, became the environmental reality; the substance of those writings was the faith in man's ability to triumph over the tragedy of his life, and in the great writings of his tenure as President, he fused the two—just as he sought, in American political and social life, to make the ideal and the reality one. The war provided him with the insight to see that ultimate unity as it expressed itself in the human tragedy of Gettysburg; and, beyond it, he saw its meaning. The result, given voice in the few remarks from the dedication platform at Gettysburg, was pure visionary human expression.

Lincoln did not become a great writer in any conventional sense, and to attempt to describe him as such is useless. Rather he became a great writer because in the truest sense he knew and understood the American experience, the microcosm of the human experience through the ages, and in a few succinct writings he was able to give that understanding focus and meaning on the rare occasions in which circumstances made that expression possible and fruitful.

Lincoln's writings are manifestations of Emerson's literary dictum that form follows idea, that truth, given free rein, would find its own means of expression. The most immediate practical writings—the stump speeches, resolutions, directives, executive orders, political letters, telegrams, and countless others, the bulk of his writings—indicate the operation of that dictum on its lowest levels as Lincoln strove for clarity and utilitarian effect. Even in satire he found the means through forms in which his barbs would be most pointed, most subtly obvious, and most effective. But the significant manifestation of Emerson's dictum lies in the three great utterances of the war years: the Gettysburg Address, the letter to Mrs. Bixby, and the Second Inaugural Address—the three works of his maturity, and the three out of the surviving million words he wrote upon which his literary reputation must ultimately be based.

[190]

In these three works Lincoln did not raise himself above the mundane and produce literature; instead, in each he attempted to make whole and articulate the essence of ideas, emotions, and bursts of insight that had suddenly found both the opportunity and the inspiration for expression. The product of a short span of time at the end of his life, they represent the culmination, the final statement of the meaning of a man, his experience, and his time; in those statements, expressions of an ultimate single meaning, Lincoln came close to and touched for a moment the only universal meaning life can possibly hold, and in those moments he achieved literary greatness.

The Gettysburg Address is the meaning of the battle and the human tragedy of the war, but it is also the meaning of the tragedy and the final triumph of human life. And in that speech Lincoln made clear the only value that human life can have, a value that transcends individual tragedy in its search for meaning beyond. Such value, an aspiration rather than a tangible end, is not individual; its substance is of the countless individual lives that point out the way and that make movement toward it possible; but its reality is the sum of the human hopes abstracted into an ideal impossible in individual terms.

The significance of these words in their position at the beginning of the end of the war, within sight of the new birth of freedom Lincoln sought, is that they illustrate Lincoln's first realization of the ultimate order beyond apparent chaos, visionary as yet, but within the realm of attainment if man had the will and the vision to see beyond the torment. The address was, in effect, a new prayer, at once demanding and exhorting, as it led his audience to look up from the graves at their feet and see the promise in the distance beyond.

In his letter to Mrs. Bixby, Lincoln captured, for a moment, out of profound compassion for a loss irreparable in an individual sense, a glimpse of that same vision, not, this time out of the anonymity of new-made, nameless graves, but out of the graves dug in a mother's heart. Intensely personal in both grief and empathy, it is no less personal in its view of what lay beyond; and the solemnity of grief is transmuted into solemn pride in the process.

These two writings are in a sense prefatory to the final statement of the second inaugural address because in it the abstracted vision is returned to tangible reality in the particularized details of the war and its aftermath and in the reality of relations among men. In its righteousness, it is humble; in its forgiveness, it finds absolution; and, in its dedication, it finds direction and meaning. The reality Lincoln found and defined is that of the American ideal, as it had been defined almost eighty years before; and he saw that—with understanding, dedication, and determination— the two would become one, union, the political reality, and liberty and equality, its spiritual counterparts, merged irretrievably in the American experience.

With these three documents as a basis, Lincoln's literary reputation is secure; without them, it would be minor. But many of the lesser works are the context out of which these have grown, just as the complexity of the man and his time gave them their depth and strength. To understand Lincoln and his work is, as Emerson recognized more than a century ago, to understand America as symbol and as reality; and his works, both major and minor, point to that understanding. Lincoln's drummer, heard faintly through the years until it reached its crescendo in the rattle of rifle fire from countless battlefields, was the heartbeat of a nation as it sought its identity, and the echoes of that drum are the rhythms of his works. As he marched to that beat from obscurity to greatness, he marched the path of his time and his people; and, as he reached the height of his greatness, he recorded what he saw and understood for those whose eyes were not so keen, whose minds were less acute, and whose voices were mute. This is the ultimate test of great writing in any age, and it provides the proof of Lincoln's greatness as man and as writer.

Notes and References

Chapter One

1. Carl Sandburg, *Abraham Lincoln: The Prairie Years* (New York, 1926), II, 356. Lincoln's biographical statement appears in *The Collected Works of Abraham Lincoln*, edited by Roy P. Basler (New Brunswick, 1953) IV, 60–67. The latter nine-volume work is cited hereafter as *The Collected Works*.

2. Frederick Jackson Turner's paper, "The Significance of the Frontier in American History," was read at a meeting of the American Historical Society in Chicago in July, 1893. It provided the major impetus toward a close examination of the impact of the frontier movement on the growth of American institutions and values.

3. For the biographical and genealogical facts of Lincoln's life and background I am indebted to Carl Sandburg, *Abraham Lincoln: The Prairie Years* and *The War Years*, 6 vols. New York, 1926 and 1939; William H. Herndon and Jesse W. Weik, *Herndon's Life of Lincoln*, edited, with introduction and notes by Paul M. Angle (Cleveland, 1949); and Benjamin P. Thomas, *Abraham Lincoln* (New York, 1952). For the interpretations of these facts I am largely responsible.

4. *The Collected Works*, I, 1.

Chapter Two

1. *The Collected Works*, I, 5. Hereafter, all citations to volume and page in this source will appear after appropriate quotations.

2. A statement attributed to Allen's son, Major Robert Allen, who had published the letter in the *Illinois State Journal* on May 10, 1865. See footnote in *The Collected Works*, I, 49.

3. "Verry" in the complimentary closing line is Lincoln's spelling. Lincoln's actual spellings are given in all quotations throughout this book, whether "correct" or not; [*sic*] is not used to verify "misspellings." Occasional interpolations are made for clarity.

Chapter Three

1. Quoted in Angle, ed., *Herndon's Life of Lincoln*, pp. 119–20.

2. For this interpretation, see Herbert J. Edwards and John E. Hankins, *Lincoln the Writer* (Orono, Maine, 1962), pp. 32–33.

3. Quoted in Carl Sandburg and Paul M. Angle, *Mary Lincoln, Wife and Widow* (New York, 1932), p. 184.

Chapter Four

1. Lincoln described his plan for the work in a letter to Andrew Johnston, a friend practicing law in Quincy, Illinois, but apparently the projected four-canto work was never completed. See *The Collected Works*, I, 367.

2. The Quincy *Whig,* April 15, 1846, quoted in *The Collected Works*, I, 371.

3. *The Collected Works*, I, 509. The words enclosed in brackets in the text of this document are those substituted by Lincoln for words in the original when he prepared it for publication in the *Congressional Globe*. See editor's note, *ibid.*, p. 501.

4. The Boston *Atlas*, September 16, 1848, quoted in *The Collected Works*, II, 5. The speech referred to is missing.

5. *The Bristol County Democrat*, September 29, 1848, quoted in *The Collected Works*, II, 6–7. This speech, too, is missing.

6. Herndon and Weik, *Life of Lincoln*, pp. 238–39.

7. *Ibid.*, p. 239.

Chapter Five

1. *The Illinois Journal*, October 5, 1854, quoted in *The Collected Works*, II, 242.

2. *The Collected Works*, II, 96–97. The letter is damaged, and bracketed words were supplied by Nicolay and Hay. See editor's note, p. 97.

3. *The Alton Weekly Courier*, June 5, 1856, quoted in *The Collected Works*, II, p. 341.

4. Herndon, p. 313.

Chapter Six

1. Paul M. Angle, editor, *Created Equal? The Complete Lincoln-Douglas Debates of 1858* (Chicago, 1958), pp. 21–22.

2. *Ibid.*, p.152.

Chapter Seven

1. The Council Bluffs *Bugle*, August 17, 1859, quoted in *The Collected Works*, III, 396. See editor's note, p. 397.

2. Stephen A. Douglas, "The Dividing Line Between Federal and Local Authority," *Harper's Magazine*, XIV (September, 1859), p. 519.

3. *Ibid.*, p. 537.

Chapter Eight

1. *The Collected Works*, IV, 190. Three versions of this farewell speech exist. This version, written in Lincoln's and Nicolay's handwritings, immediately after the train departed, is most immediate. See editor's notes, *ibid.*, p. 191.

2. Letter to Brigadier General Samuel R. Curtis, October 7, 1861, in *The Collected Works*, IV, 549.

Chapter Nine

1. Letter to James C. Conkling, August 26, 1863, in *The Collected Works*, VI, 410.

2. *The Collected Works*, VII, 23. This is the final text, the so-called Bliss Copy. See editor's notes in *ibid.*, pp. 17–23, for a detailed textual discussion of the various texts extant.

Selected Bibliography

PRIMARY SOURCES

1. The Published Writings of Abraham Lincoln

The Collected Works of Abraham Lincoln. Edited by Roy P. Basler. Marian Delores Pratt and Lloyd A. Dunlap, assistant editors. In nine volumes. New Brunswick, New Jersey: Rutgers University Press, 1953.

The Complete Works of Abraham Lincoln. Edited by John G. Nicolay and John Hay. New and enlarged edition in ten volumes. Harrogate, Tennessee: Lincoln Memorial University, 1894.

Created Equal? The Complete Lincoln-Douglas Debates of 1858. Edited and with an introduction by Paul M. Angle. Chicago: The University of Chicago Press, 1958.

In The Name of the People: Speeches and Writings of Lincoln and Douglas in the Ohio Campaign of 1859. Edited, with an introduction, by Harry V. Jaffa and Robert W. Johannsen. Columbus: The Ohio State University Press, 1959.

2. Outstanding Collections of Manuscripts

The Library of Congress Collection.

The Herndon-Weik Collection in The Library of Congress.

The Robert Todd Lincoln Collection of the Papers of Abraham Lincoln in the Library of Congress.

The Illinois State Historical Library, Springfield, Illinois.

The Lincoln National Life Foundation, Fort Wayne, Indiana.

SECONDARY SOURCES

1. Books

BARTON, WILLIAM E. *Lincoln At Gettysburg.* Indianapolis: The Bobbs-Merrill Co., 1930. Traces the circumstances of the ceremony and address.

————. *The Lineage of Lincoln.* Indianapolis: The Bobbs-Merrill Co., 1929. Lincoln family genealogy.

BASLER, ROY P. *The Lincoln Legend.* Boston: The Houghton-Mifflin Co., 1935. Imaginative interpretations of Lincoln. A basic study.

BEVERIDGE, ALBERT J. *Abraham Lincoln.* Boston: The Houghton-Mifflin Co., 1928. Good, unfortunately unfinished biography.

CHARNWOOD, LORD. *Abraham Lincoln.* New York: Henry Holt and Co., 1917. One-volume biography superseded by Thomas.

CURRENT, RICHARD N. *The Lincoln Nobody Knows.* New York: McGraw-Hill, Inc., 1958. Study of myths, legends, and competing accounts.

CURRENT, RICHARD N. and JAMES G. RANDALL. *Lincoln the President: Last Full Measure.* New York: Dodd, Mead and Co., 1955. Close, penetrating study of the final months.

DODGE, DANIEL K. *Abraham Lincoln: The Evolution of His Literary Style.* University of Illinois Studies, Vol. I, No. 1 (May, 1900). Early stylistic study.

DONALD, DAVID. *Lincoln's Herndon.* New York: Alfred A. Knopf, 1948. Standard study of Herndon.

————. *Lincoln Reconsidered.* New York: Alfred A. Knopf, 1956. Examination of competing issues and interpretations.

EDWARDS, HERBERT J. and JOHN E. HANKINS. *Lincoln the Writer.* "University of Maine Studies," Second Series, No. 76: Orono, Maine, 1962. Interesting but somewhat effusive and eulogistic study.

HARKNESS, DAVID J. and R. GERALD MCMURTRY. *Lincoln's Favorite Poets.* Knoxville: The University of Tennessee Press, 1959. Interesting anthology.

HERNDON, WILLIAM H. and JESSE W. WEIK. *Abraham Lincoln: The True Story of a Great Life.* New York: D. Appleton and Co., 1892. Herndon's classic study.

————. *Herndon's Lincoln.* Edited, with an introduction and notes by Paul M. Angle. Cleveland: Fine Editions Press, 1949. Combined, an excellent study of Herndon on Lincoln.

HOLLAND, JOSIAH G. *The Life of Abraham Lincoln.* Springfield, Mass.: Gurdon Bill, 1866. Interesting early study.

HOWELLS, WILLIAM DEAN. *The Lives and Speeches of Abraham Lincoln and Hannibal Hamlin.* Columbus: Follett and Foster, 1860. Standard campaign biography.

LEWIS, LLOYD. *Myths after Lincoln.* New York: Harcourt, Brace and Co., 1929. Good examination of myth and reality.

MEARNS, DAVID C. *The Lincoln Papers.* New York: Doubleday and Co., 1948. Story of the Mearns Collection.

MESERVE, FREDERICK H. and CARL SANDBURG. *The Photographs of Abraham Lincoln.* New York: Harcourt, Brace and Co., 1944. Standard collection of photographs.

MIERS, EARL SCHENCK, editor-in-chief. *Lincoln Day by Day: A Chronology, 1809–1865.* Washington: Lincoln Sesquicentennial Commission, 1960. 3 vols. Exhaustive, definitive study.

MITGANG, HERBERT. *Lincoln as They Saw Him.* New York: Rinehart and Co., 1956. Contemporary views of Lincoln.

NEVINS, ALLAN. *The Emergence of Lincoln.* New York: Charles Scribner's Sons, 1950. 2 vols. The background and setting.

————. *The Statesmanship of the Civil War.* New York: The Macmillan Co., 1953. Insight into responses to demands.

————. *The War for the Union.* New York: Charles Scribner's Sons, 1959. The war years.

NICOLAY, JOHN G. and JOHN HAY. *Abraham Lincoln, A History.* New York: The Century Co., 1886. Interesting comparison with Herndon.

RANDALL, JAMES G. *Lincoln the President: Springfield to Gettysburg.* New York: Dodd, Mead and Co., 1946. 2 vols. The crucial late formative years.

————. *Lincoln the President: Midstream.* New York: Dodd, Mead and Co., 1952. The dangerous mid-war period.

RANDALL, RUTH PAINTER. *The Courtship of Mr. Lincoln.* Boston: Little, Brown and Co., 1957. Opposes Herndon.

————. *Lincoln's Sons.* Boston: Little, Brown and Co., 1955. A touching study.

————. *Mary Lincoln: Biography of a Marriage.* Boston: Little, Brown and Co., 1953. Again disputes Herndon's view.

RIDDLE, DONALD W. *Congressman Abraham Lincoln.* Urbana: University of Illinois Press, 1957. Intensive study of the years in Washington.

————. *Lincoln Runs for Congress.* New Brunswick: Rutgers University Press, 1948. Study of the campaign.

ROBINSON, LUTHER E. *Abraham Lincoln as a Man of Letters.* New York: G. P. Putnam's Sons, 1923. Noncritical literary history.

SANDBURG, CARL. *Abraham Lincoln: The Prairie Years.* New York: Harcourt, Brace and Co., 1926. 2 vols. Exhaustive but undocumented study.

————. *Abraham Lincoln: The War Years.* New York: Harcourt, Brace and Co., 1936. 4 vols. Continuation of the former in the same style.

———— and PAUL M. ANGLE. *Mary Lincoln, Wife and Widow.* New York: Harcourt, Brace and Co., 1932. A study contrary to many of Herndon's assertions.

THOMAS, BENJAMIN P. *Abraham Lincoln.* New York: Alfred A. Knopf, 1952. Standard one-volume biography.

Selected Bibliography

2. Articles and Essays

ANDERSON, DAVID D. "Abraham Lincoln, Man of Letters," *University College Quarterly*, XII (January, 1967). A summary statement.

————. "Emerson and Lincoln," *The Lincoln Herald*, LX (Winter, 1958). Traces the emergence of Emerson's admiration for Lincoln.

————. "The Man Who Nominated Lincoln," *The Northwest Ohio Quarterly*, XXXI (Summer, 1959). Identifies Robert K. Enos as the man responsible for switching Ohio's votes to Lincoln.

————. "Sherwood Anderson's Use of the Lincoln Theme," *The Lincoln Herald*, LXIV (Spring, 1962). Explores Anderson's use of Lincoln material in fiction and in a biographical fragment.

BARZUN, JACQUES. "Lincoln the Literary Genius," *The Saturday Evening Post*, CCXXXI (February 14, 1959). Published as a book by the Shori Private Press, Evanston, Ill., 1961. Interesting general study.

BASLER, ROY P. "Abraham Lincoln—Artist," *North American Review*, CCXLV (Spring, 1938). General study of techniques.

————. "Abraham Lincoln's Rhetoric," *American Literature*, XI (May, 1939). Significant rhetorical study.

BERKELMAN, ROBERT. "Lincoln's Interest in Shakespeare," *Shakespeare Quarterly*, II (October, 1951). Traces development of interest.

NICOLAY, JOHN G. "Lincoln's Gettysburg Address," *The Century Magazine*, XLVII (February, 1894). Discusses the texts.

————. "Lincoln's Literary Experiments," *The Century Magazine*, VLVII (April, 1894). Interesting and important insights for the time.

THOMAS, BENJAMIN P. "Lincoln's Humor—An Analysis," Abraham Lincoln Association Papers (Springfield, Ill., 1936). Examines the humor critically.

WILSON, EDMUND. "Abraham Lincoln: The Union as Religious Mysticism." *Eight Essays*. New York: Doubleday and Co., 1954. Perceptive review essay.

Index

(References to Lincoln's works will be found under the author's name.)